THE COST
OF
CARELESSNESS

THE COST
Of
CARELESSNESS

JEFF BOOTH
WITH
TERRI BOOTH

XULON PRESS

Jeff & Terri Booth are the founders and Lead Pastors of Freedom Worship Center Omaha. They have served in various ministry positions in Indiana and Nebraska. Jeff has a heart for the nations and has experienced the privilege of ministering in many nations. Together, Jeff and Terri have written and recorded many worship songs that are used in corporate worship settings here and abroad.

Jeff married his high school sweetheart Terri. They are blessed with sons Jevan, Jackson, and Jadin, along with daughter Jordan, who has a son Harrison with her husband Lucas.

Connect with Jeff:
Twitter: @JeffLBooth
Facebook: Jeff Booth
www.fwcomaha.org

Xulon Press
2301 Lucien Way #415
Maitland, FL 32751
407.339.4217
www.xulonpress.com

© 2017 by Jeff Booth Terri Booth

Unless otherwise indicated, Scripture quotations taken from the Holy Bible, New International Version (NIV). Copyright © 1973, 1978, 1984, 2011 by Biblica, Inc.™. Used by permission. All rights reserved, the New King James Version (NKJV). Copyright © 1982 by Thomas Nelson, Inc. Used by permission. All rights reserved, the Holy Bible, New Living Translation (NLT). Copyright ©1996, 2004, 2007 by Tyndale House Foundation. Used by permission of Tyndale House Publishers, Inc.

Printed in the United States of America.

ISBN-13: 978-1-54561-338-2

Table Of Contents

Preface

I had the privilege of being raised_by my mother who taught me the principles and values of God's word found on the pages of what we know as the Holy Bible. My earliest memories are of being fascinated by various preachers and evangelists that my mother would position me under who could teach God's word in ways that people could understand and live out in their daily lives.

By the time I was nine years old, I believe I had a call on my life to preach the Gospel message. My older brothers John and Jim could sing and play various instruments, and I wanted to be just like them, so I followed in their footsteps. My brother John would take me to nursing homes when I was 12–13 years old, and he would have me sing hymns and preach a message to those who would listen.

My brothers used to sing all the time at our home church as well as at other churches, and my brother Jim actually traveled with a group for a while. I really wanted to be able to preach God's word and use music to communicate this Good News.

Before I graduated high school, I joined a Christian rock band and began playing around the state of Indiana at coffee houses, churches, festivals, high schools, and anywhere they would let us. I really wanted to be a full time musician. I enjoyed writing songs and the collaborative process with a band.

Over time our band went from 7 members to 4, to 3, to 2, and then it was no more. That season would close, and God would use every bit of it for my next season. I need to give some thanks to Gary Bone, Doug Stanfield, Tony Huff, Gary Staggs, Jed Morehouse, and Vern Vanderkleed for their friendship and for the journey we shared together for many years as a band as well as serving in our local church.

I eventually went into full time ministry as a youth pastor, then worship leader, and today I pastor an inner city church in Omaha, Nebraska, where my family and I are enjoying God's blessings upon our ministry and on our family.

Throughout my life and ministry, I have been amazed at how Christians, particularly in America, view prayer and specifically how God answers prayer.

It seems that we just tell God what we want, and then He is supposed to answer promptly to our requests with more than what we've asked for. Don't get me wrong; I have experienced answers to prayers that have been for my needs and desires. *However, is prayer really about getting what we want, or is prayer about God getting what He wants?*

Throughout my life experiences, I've faced job layoffs, financial needs, health issues, marital difficulties, ministry disappointments, and situations that I'm sure you have faced before. But I've never had an experience where I felt powerless to make it if God chose not to make a way for me than what I faced in April of 2016.

I came face to face with the question, "What if God doesn't answer my prayer the way I'm asking Him to answer it?"

And I had to wrestle with the concern, "What do I do while I wait for the answer to my prayer?"

In other words, the space between a prayer prayed and the answer to the prayer could be a long time. What do you do in the space between? Do you get angry with God? Do you turn from God? Do you run to God?

That is the basis for the book that you are reading right now. I hope that your faith will be strengthened, and that you find that *while you are waiting God is working.*

Remember: Don't doubt in the dark times of your life what you know to be true in the light.

The Good Life

I had the time of my life serving as youth pastor at First Assembly of God in Lafayette, Indiana, where I had served five previous youth pastors in a variety of ways. Two of my best friends were associate and senior pastors of the church, and my secretary used to call us the "Dream Team." We had a blast.

Our youth ministry doubled in size by the grace of God, and for four years we saw God touch young people who later went into full time ministry and global missions work. It was a great season of our lives where our three small children pretty much lived in youth ministry with us.

My wife was an elementary teacher at the academy based out of our church, and we really loved the ministry God had called us to. However, we both received a word from the Lord while at separate conferences that revealed our time there was coming to a close.

Isaiah 42:9 (ASV) says, "See, the former things have taken place, and new things I declare; before they spring into being I announce them to you."

We serve an amazing God who gives us warnings and direction about the path we are to take. God was instructing my wife and I from Genesis 12 where He tells Abram in verse 1 (NIV), "The Lord had said to Abram, 'Leave your country, your people and your father's household and go to the land I will show you.'"

After the process of much prayer, seeking the Lord, and seeking the counsel of our pastoral leadership, we resigned as youth pastors in August of 1999 without knowing where we were going. We just knew that in order to move into the new place and plans that God had prepared for us in this season of our lives, we had to let go of the old. So that's exactly what we did.

We had just completed restoring an 80 year old home on three acres with trees and a barn, and God was asking us to sell it and step out into the unknown. It was scary, and in my natural mind it didn't make sense. However, I've always found it to be wisdom to follow God even when it doesn't make sense.

We received offers to become worship pastors in Colorado, California, and Illinois. We pressed toward God's leading but just didn't have peace about any of these places. In February 2000, I was traveling for ministry and my wife called me and told me that she took a call from a pastor in Omaha, Nebraska, and as she shared with me the conversation they had, we had no doubt that this was where God was leading us to.

We visited Omaha Glad Tidings Church in March, and we had the peace of God that this was our new home. We loved the church and the staff. We had a sense that God was already doing something special here and He was inviting us to be a part of it. Our interview went extremely well, and I went on staff as their worship pastor while my wife finished up the school year with our kids back in Indiana.

The transition to Omaha was difficult because our lives had been spent in Indiana and our roots were deep. But we made the move, and I remember hearing the voice of God speak to my wife and I that this move was more about our children than it was about our ministry. I'm so thankful we made the move. The blessing of the Lord is evident in the opportunities and development of our kids. Our obedience to step into "the new" resulted in unbelievable blessings for our children.

Our daughter met her husband here, and we've been blessed with our first grandchild. Our sons have developed ministry gifts and have built amazing relationships that would not have happened if we had remained in the comfort of our hometown.

Our oldest son has developed leadership skills that have resulted in great influence with youth and parents.

We have a son who has worked in the White House and the State Department, and all of our kids have traveled to many different countries to communicate the Gospel. I might have to stop right here and give a praise break for the goodness of the Lord in the lives of my kids!

In August of 2002, we welcomed our fourth child into the world. Our Husker surprise was a bouncing baby boy to join our other two sons and our daughter. God's favor is on this child as well. We are most blessed.

It's important that you go where God calls you. There are more beautiful places that we had opportunities to go, but I'm so thankful that we followed the Lord's leading to Omaha.

We have experienced the blessing of God in our lives, and one of the greatest blessings involves the relationships that we have developed. One of those relationships would soon become much more than a mere ministry acquaintance.

Acknowledgments

From April 1st to June 25th, 1945 in the battle for Okinawa, 287,000 troops of the Tenth U.S. Army battled fiercely against 130,000 soldiers of the Japanese 32nd Army. The 82-day campaign was significant to ending World War II.

Japan had lost more than 77,000 soldiers, and the Allies had suffered more than 65,000 casualties, including 14,000 dead. Both sides paid an extremely high price. "It was a scene straight out of hell. There is no other way to describe it," recalls Higa Tomiko, then a seven-year-old girl, who survived the battle.

My uncle Andy Cooper was a marine fighting during this battle on the island of Okinawa. He was one of the U.S. soldiers who fought valiantly; he was also one of the fortunate ones that came home when many others did not. He was pretty amazing to me. I can remember as a little boy when he would visit and would play our piano. I loved watching him play boogie-woogie style. I have come to realize that he was more of an influence to me when it came to music than I had thought.

Uncle Andy worked for NASA, and before retiring he spent much of his career training and instructing in the Middle East.

He passed away many years ago, but his sacrifice and service along with thousands of other brave soldiers have made it possible for me to minister the Gospel of Christ in Okinawa many times since 2001.

The Bible says in John 12:24 (ESV), "Truly, truly, I say to you, unless a grain of wheat falls into the earth and dies, it remains alone; but if it dies, it bears much fruit."

Jesus went onto say in John 15:13, "Greater love has no one than this, that someone lay down his life for his friends."

Thank you to Uncle Andy Cooper and all the brave soldiers for their sacrifice that has produced much fruit, and by the grace of God will continue to produce. One day I'll see you again and we can walk streets of gold together and maybe find an old piano somewhere so we can jam.

I would like to thank Dave Boyer for introducing me to Bishop James Whitaker. I also want to thank him for being an example of what a Godly man looks like as a husband and father. Thank you, Dave, for your dedicated service to our country.

Thank you to my amazing kids—Jordan, Jevan, Jackson, Jadin, and my son-in-law, Lucas. I'm not sure there is anything more rewarding than to see your kids grow up and begin to live out their God-given purpose and to see them love God with all of their heart, soul, mind, and strength. I'm proud of the people you all have become, and of what your futures will bring. April of 2016 revealed your character, maturity, and strength in the midst of testing. I love you all, and I am most blessed to be your father.

Thank you to Bishop James and Gloria Whitaker who have taught me much about loving, giving, serving, selflessness, Kingdom-mindedness, and much more. God has provided me with true friends in the two of you. Both of you model and imitate Christ in everyday living. You have raised disciples all around the world who are your sons and daughters in the faith, and you advance the heart of Jesus throughout the nations. "Thank you" doesn't quite seem to cover my heartfelt sentiments toward you. I love you both! Thank you!

Joshua Whitaker, you were the first one to visit me, and I'll never forget your encouragement and determination to do whatever it would take to see that I was okay. You are an amazing man of God, husband, father, and son. You are a reflection of your father and mother, but ultimately you are an amazing reflection of our Heavenly Father. Thank you for being there when I really needed someone.

To the family of Freedom Worship Center Omaha: I cannot put into words how much I love you and count it a privilege to be your pastor. Thank you for your love and support for my family and me. I LOVE MY CHURCH!

To my mother, Rheeta Booth: Thanks, mom, for giving me such a love for God's word and His presence. It's what sustained me then, and sustains me still. Thank you for your sacrifices throughout the years to give me opportunities that I never could have imagined. I'm proud to be your son. I love you, Mom!

To my family—the Booths, Bowmans, Trujillos, Grimeses, and Justices—I am most blessed because of the family God has given to me. Love you all!

Thank you to my brothers John and Jim and my sister Missy for your love and support as well as your investment in my life in so many ways.

To Annette M. Eddie-Callagain: What a blessing to see your smiling face when I needed it most! Thank you for giving of your time and expertise to make sure I was all right. What an amazing act of God to position you to be in the right place at the right time. We serve an incredible God. God bless you!

This book is dedicated to the love of my life. Just when I think we've experienced it all, we find ourselves being tested, tried, and sharpened by the journey of life. Thank you for your unconditional love and commitment to serve Jesus no matter what He asks of us. You are filled with such grace and wisdom, and I'm extremely blessed to spend my life with you. 2017 marks our 35th wedding anniversary, and I am most blessed to call you my wife, mother of my children, confidante, and my very best friend. I love you! (Let's go to Hawaii soon!)

Chapter 1

Great Co-Mission Conference

On April 6, 2016, I boarded my flight from Omaha to Okinawa. I was filled with excitement to see Bishop James Whitaker and some other friends I had not seen in almost seven years. My good friend Bishop Whitaker had gone through some serious health issues and I really wanted to visit him to encourage him, as he has been such an encouragement to my life.

I met Bishop James E. Whitaker from Okinawa, Japan in 2001 for the first time. Dave Boyer was one of the deacons at our church and he had been stationed in Okinawa serving in the Air Force. Dave and his family attended Zion Christian Fellowship where Bishop Whitaker was the pastor. It was through Dave that Bishop Whitaker came to our church in Omaha to minister, and our great friendship began. As they say, the rest is history.

Bishop Whitaker and I hit it off right away, and that started an annual journey each March for me to attend the Great Co-Mission Conference in Okinawa. At this conference, I have met many powerful men and women of God. This is an environment where the heart of Bishop Whitaker was on full display as he welcomed ministers and missionaries from all over the world to gather and celebrate what God was doing in their part of the world.

Bishop is known as the "Black Japanese" because he is African-American and speaks fluent Japanese. He has great favor throughout Japan, as well as in many parts of the world. He is full of life, faith, and love for Jesus that moves him to take action wherever there might be a need. He never faces a challenge for which he doesn't already see God's plan of victory and provision. He is a man full of faith in God.

Zion Christian Fellowship is the platform where ministry flows for Bishop Whitaker. The church is mixed with Japanese and military because of the United States' military presence on the island.

From planting churches in other nations and providing shoes to teenagers in Jamaican prisons to providing medical attention to the Filipino's, you will find Bishop and Gloria Whitaker loving and leading people to Jesus. I love to be around people like this, whose faith is big.

At the Great Co-Mission Conference, I've met men and women of God from around the world who are amazing people of faith. I was humbled to be a part of this great conference where many powerful leaders gathered to celebrate the Kingdom of God.

It is in these environments that the Holy Spirit speaks fresh instructions, and it is in this environment that you get a glimpse of what the Father is doing in the earth.

With ministries attending from Jamaica, South Africa, Japan, India and the Philippines as well as ministries from the States, my vision has been enlarged.

Remember, I'm just a boy from Indiana that said yes to Jesus and had no clue where His journey would take me.

Allow me to back up a bit to explain why I have made many trips to Okinawa in the first place. In 1999, I was "infected" with the "missions bug." I had no plan to travel outside of the United States until a businessman named Joe Livesay asked me to go to New Delhi, India with him. Since that initial mission trip, God has led me to many nations to sing, preach, teach, encourage, and serve the Church and its leaders. I'm amazed at all God can do through a simple, "Yes, Lord."

If we don't step outside of our box and walk through the doors God opens for us, we will never have an expanded vision of the Kingdom. God wants you to see beyond your neighborhood, city, and church. The truth is, if we choose to remain where we are and not step into the new, we will ultimately find ourselves in a place of irrelevance.

Now, you don't have to travel far from the "Good Life" of Nebraska to experience people who have great need. Simply visit one of the Native American reservations that are close to us. Your heart will break as God's heart breaks for the First Nations people of our land who suffer from alcoholism, suicide, and economic inequities. Your eyes are quickly opened to a world that God loves and that His heart is close to. You will never know God's heart if you don't step outside of your comfort zone to see for yourself.

The goal is not to merely see, but to move from seeing into action through a compassionate heart that desires people be impacted by the Gospel of Jesus Christ.

The community I minister in is North Omaha. It is an area many people tend to stay away from. Some statistics show that Omaha, Nebraska has more millionaires per capita than any other city in the U.S., and the unemployment rate is way below the national average. Yet children in my community go hungry every night. Unemployment is in the high double digits in North Omaha.

Though we are seeing economic and housing developments in our community, the inequity is visible and real with the lack of jobs that can sustain families. Crime is a real issue along with gang activity, alcohol, and drug addiction. Hopelessness abounds for many people in my community.

Hopelessness causes people to live lifestyles that they were never meant to live and to experience addictions that destroy their lives. People without hope will do just about anything because there is no vision for their future. In short, there seems to be no way out of the predicament they are born into.

Someone once said, "To the one without hope, consequences mean nothing." Crime, violence, and murder are common in a community where there is no hope.

Our responsibility as believers in Jesus Christ is to go into the dark places and shine the light of God's love through acts of compassion. We have a responsibility to bring hope to the hopeless and peace to troubled hearts. There is a responsibility to love the unlovable, because that's who and what we once were before we met Jesus.

If you will step outside of your comfort zone, your heart will be moved to action to see that the Gospel impacts every tribe, every nation, and every tongue that will receive it.

Step out of your boat and walk on water! Don't live safely. One of the most famous missionaries, Jim Elliott, once wrote, "When it's your time to die, make sure that's all you have left to do." That's how I want to go out. I want to complete my assignment so all I have to do is step into the Father's presence and hear, "Well done."

Well, back to Bishop. You see, everything that Bishop Whitaker is a part of is to see that "nations" know the love of Jesus. It is a beautiful celebration of the Kingdom advancing in these nations. The Great Co-Mission Conference features music, word, dance, and testimonies from various ministries around the world in their own language and culture. It's a small picture of what heaven will be like.

In 2010, my wife and I felt a change in our ministry, so we resigned our position at Glad Tidings and became lead pastors of Freedom Church in the inner city, complete with its declining membership and building/financial woes. We renamed it Freedom Worship Center Omaha, shifted its focus and revitalized the facility. Due to the demands of a new church, my traveling was limited. I had made a couple of short trips to Cuba and one to Burkina Faso, West Africa; however, I had not been able to return to Okinawa for about seven years.

The church began to grow and we established a leadership team that gave me the ability to begin to travel again as opportunities were presented. When I received the news that Bishop Whitaker had been dealing with some serious health issues, I knew that I needed to return to Okinawa to see him at the next Great Co-Mission Conference.

I bought my ticket and let Bishop know that I was going to see him soon. I could tell he was happy, and I was happy to be seeing him again after so long.

I arrived in Okinawa on April 7, and the conference began the following day. The conference was amazing as usual with music, testimonies, and the preaching of God's Word by Japanese pastors and other guests from around the world.

On the final night of the conference, the Lord gave me a prophetic Word through Pastor Alex from Brazil. The Word from the Lord was, "A greater anointing is coming on you, a miracle is coming, and new doors are opening for you." I received the Word and toward the end of the service Pastor Alex came back to me and emphasized that "'new doors are opening for you."

As I left the meeting on Sunday night, I was encouraged and excited to see how this prophetic Word would play out in my life. A greater anointing would require greater responsibility, and I was excited about seeing a miracle take place in my life as we could sure use a few miracles! To have the Lord tell me that new doors were about to open was pretty exciting as well. I wondered how this Word would play out in my life, and I was anxious to share it with my wife when I returned to Omaha.

I spent the night on Kadena Air Force base, but didn't really sleep well. I was up most of the night, so I read a little bit to pass the time. When morning came, my driver arrived and I was taken to the airport for my departure.

This is always a bittersweet time as we say goodbye to friends, but we're also anxious to get home to family. As I said my goodbyes and checked in at the airport, Bishop Whitaker prayed with me and then had to go meet up with several others from Zion Christian Fellowship in another location of the airport because they were going to the Philippines for a week of medical mission and a pastor's conference as they do each year.

I told Bishop I loved him and would continue praying for his health, and it was at this point that God would open a "new door."

Chapter 2

A New Door

It was good to spend these days with Bishop Whitaker and his family. The conference was a blessing, and I really enjoyed seeing how the ministry in Okinawa was stronger than ever. My heart was overjoyed to see Bishop doing well in his physical health. His mind and his spirit are always strong, and he was such an encouragement to me during this visit.

On Monday, April 11th I met Bishop at the airport to say our goodbyes and to let him know I would continue to pray for him. I checked in and got my boarding pass then headed to security. I felt that I was an encouragement to Bishop, and I was also blessed by the conference and now I was really ready to get home to my wife, kids, and brand new grandson. It's a long flight, so I just wanted to board, and perhaps sleep most of the flight.

I took my shoes off and placed my carry-on bag on the conveyor belt to be examined as usual, and as my carry-on bag went through the machine the airport officials pulled it off and asked if they could run my bag through a second time. I agreed without question.

On the second time through, the security personnel asked if I would step aside and open my bag for them to do a further examination. This was odd, but once again, it was no problem. I did what they asked me to do. However, I did notice that as I opened my bag they had called for the airport police to join them. People around me were staring at me, and obviously they could understand what the security personnel were saying, but I couldn't. Something was up, and I began to have a level of concern that I had never experienced before.

When the police arrived, they were examining my bag and as they looked deep inside a pocket where I keep my Bible, glasses, and pens one of the officers reached in and pulled out a single bullet. It was at this point that things got a little intense.

The police and security personnel began talking to each other more, and they would look at me but I had no idea what their concern was.

As a little background, at various times I will use this carry-on bag to hold my personal weapon and ammunition to go to the shooting range, and I thought I had cleaned my bag out completely. However, I was wrong. I was very wrong.

There was no translator, but with all the commotion and pointing I could tell I was in serious trouble. This was no little matter to them.

You see, in Japan, there is zero tolerance for weapons. The two things Japanese culture does not tolerate are weapons and drugs. I wasn't in America anymore, and I had nobody to come to my defense for what I thought was a simple mistake on my part. There is no Second Amendment in Japan.

A smiling airline employee took my ticket, and it was interesting that one officer simply asked me to follow him upstream through the long line of people who were putting their bags on the belt to be x-rayed. He didn't hold my arm, and no other officers assisted us as we made our way through the crowd and out the door in front of the departure drop off in front of the airport. He just walked quickly in front of me expecting I was right with him. As we finally made our way into the airport police station, he asked me to sit down.

I was getting concerned because I no longer had my ticket for my return flight home, and nobody in the police station would answer me when I tried to inquire about what they were doing. I got up from my seat and leaned over the counter to try and get someone to tell me what in the world was going on, but no one responded to me. What was happening behind the scene was that they were waiting on detectives and a translator to arrive in the airport police station so they could begin to interrogate me.

It was apparent I was not going home that day. It seemed like an eternity, but after several minutes the police officer motioned for me to come behind the counter, down a hall, and into a small room. There was a small table where they asked me to sit down, and on the other side of the table a man came in carrying a briefcase and sat across from me. He didn't smile at me or introduce himself to me. He looked concerned, and waited for the detectives to give him instructions for me.

It didn't take long for two detectives to enter the room. The detectives stood over me and asked if they could inspect my bag, and once again I did not oppose them. They began a brief interrogation of me. After just a few questions that I answered, the translator who was sitting across from me at the table politely informed me that I was now under arrest for Illegal Possession of Firearms / Swords, even though they only found one round of 9mm ammunition in my carry-on bag. Their thought was that if there was a bullet in my bag then there must be a weapon somewhere.

I was instructed to stand up so they could put handcuffs on me. My heart began to race as I stood up and they put handcuffs on me. Once they had me secured, they hurried me down a hallway into a waiting vehicle. I began to panic a bit. I thought, "There is no way this is happening to me! I've never been arrested." The only time I've been in jail was to minister to people who had been arrested.

The police vehicle hurried through traffic with lights flashing and sirens blasting. I was humiliated and distraught. It seemed like an eternity, but it was only a 15–20 minute drive to the Tomigusuku Police Station Detention Facility where I was about to experience a long interrogation.

We arrived at the detention center where several officers were waiting when the car arrived, and several officers escorted me into the building through various hallways and finally into a small room. In this room they began the process of booking me, searching me, and further interrogation.

"What is going on? This cannot be happening to me! It's only one bullet!" I thought. I flew from Omaha, to Denver, to Tokyo and onto Okinawa with the same bag and nobody questioned me at any of these locations. How could this be happening to me now?

As they interrogated me, I explained to them that in my country I have a permit to carry a weapon and that my weapon and ammunition are sometimes in this bag. I showed them my concealed-carry permit. I desperately tried to tell them that I never saw this bullet, and would never have tried to bring a weapon or ammunition to another country. It was a mistake and careless oversight on my part. They showed no sympathy or mercy despite my explanation.

Off and on for the next twelve hours I was "interviewed" through a translator in a small, hot room. I was painfully aware at this point that I was guilty until proven innocent. The detectives would ask me the same questions over and over, and then word them a different way trying to trip me into giving a different answer. It was frustrating, and it began to take a toll on my mind and emotions.

They would question me extensively, and then they would put documents in front of me and ask me to sign. I was signing my name to documents, but I could not tell if they would help me or hurt me. I was just being honest, forth-right, and to the point so I thought that they would understand and let me get back to the airport and go home.

You know that feeling deep in your gut that tells you something doesn't smell right? That thing inside of you that tells you something is not right? I had that feeling big time with the detectives who questioned me. I didn't trust them. They seemed deceitful. I felt like they relished an opportunity to take an American down, and they were going to take full advantage of it. I was not convinced they were on the up and up.

I had a real concern that the translator was not translating my statements correctly. I just did not know what was really going on or what I should do. My thought was to just cooperate and they would release me to go back to the airport so I could go home,

The detectives informed me of my charge and told me that I could not speak to my wife or anyone. I could not call Bishop or anyone from the church to let them know of my situation. My heart sank to the pit of my stomach. "This cannot be happening," I thought. "I'm halfway around the world in jail, and nobody knows it."

I begged the detectives to call my wife to save her the trauma, but they did not want to do that. They said over and over that they could not do that. After several requests, one investigator told me that he would call her. To be honest, I thought he was lying to me, but I felt some peace and satisfaction thinking that maybe he would call my wife and let her know I was okay. I just wanted her to know I was okay, and not to worry. I thought, "We'll get through this somehow. God will help us."

The detectives told me that they would inform the United States Consulate in Japan to send a representative to speak with me who would in turn contact my family to let them know what was happening with me.

This was the beginning of a most difficult time of discouragement and darkness in my life.

"I made one mistake in not cleaning my bag out completely before I made this trip, and it's going to cost me dearly," I thought. It was becoming clear to me that this one, small, seemingly insignificant, careless act on my part would have a high price attached to it.

Chapter 3

Night Of Discouragement

Upon arrival at the jail, I was searched thoroughly and my luggage was examined in detail with me present. Every item in my luggage and carry-on bag was itemized and written down in a document. It seemed like this took forever, and it sealed up the truth that this was really happening to me. I was in jail, and I had no idea when I would be released.

My money was counted, and I signed documents to secure them as my personal belongings. I had to change into different clothes in front of the guards. They basically handed me a pair of sweat pants, a t-shirt, and a pair of flip-flops in exchange for my clothing.

Once my clothes were changed, they went through a detailed process of handcuffing me. There were always two guards to secure me, and a third would be brought in once secured to examine me to make sure I was secured properly. I was secured in such a way that I couldn't scratch my nose if I needed to. I was then escorted out of the room through another door and into an area that had three cells in it.

As I examined my surroundings, I noticed the three cells; they took me to the center cell and opened the door. The handcuffs were removed from me, and I was instructed to remove my flip-flops before entering the cell. As they removed my handcuffs, I noticed that the two cells on either side of me had four to five men in them, and the cell I was held in had two men in it.

The cell was approximately 8' X 10' with wrestling mats on the floor and a restroom in the corner.

As I entered the cell, I was greeted with stares from the two men who were already in the cell. They stared at me as if to size me up. I returned the stare, as I could not tell whether they would be friendly or not.

I walked past the two men, found a corner in the back of the cell to sit down, and my heart raced. My mind raced. This was not in my plans, but I was definitely not in control of anything at this point. Maybe that's what God wanted: Him in total control, and my full surrender.

Here I was some 10,000 miles away from home sitting in a Japanese jail with no hope of going home anytime soon. The situation was entirely more than I could handle. My thoughts were with my wife and family. I could not imagine what they were going through. So much was unknown, and not having any accurate information can wear on your mind.

The massive steel door closed behind me, and I was in a situation I had never experienced before. As I examined my surroundings, I looked to my left to see a short but large man with tattoos all over his body. He stared me down just about as much as I stared him down, trying to determine if he would be friendly or not. I noticed right away that his pinky finger was cut off, which I knew was a sign of someone who was at one time involved in the Japanese

Mafia. He kind of grinned and nodded at me to say hello as I turned to see the other man in the cell.

The other man was a bit younger and had a grin pinned to his face along with a constant laugh. Anything the tattoo man would say caused this younger man to laugh, giggle, and snicker. His behavior was unsettling to say the least. Was he insane? What was he in here for? This was too much to take in.

Because I didn't know their names, in my mind I quickly named the first man Shrek, and the other man Donkey. Tattoo man was built like Shrek, so that fit. And the other man was Donkey because he just seemed to laugh and giggle all the time.

I would discover that Shrek was a local who apparently liked to beat people up, so he was somewhat of a regular in this jail. Donkey was from Vietnam, and I don't know how he ended up in Okinawa or what he did to get arrested.

Shrek and Donkey talked among themselves a lot, and I felt quite left out because I simply couldn't understand their language. Shrek could speak a few words in English, like McDonald's, Sylvester Stallone, Burger King, and A&W Root Beer.

Shrek worked really hard to ask why I was in jail. I held my hand out like a gun, and Shrek about freaked out. I tried to explain that I just had a bullet but not the gun, and he assured me that it was no big deal and I would be out in three days. Somehow, we began to communicate with each other. It's amazing how you can talk when you don't know the same verbal language.

Shrek took a liking to me and would try to communicate to the guards what he thought I wanted to eat for my meals. He would even give me some of his chicken tenders and any food that was somewhat American. No matter what they brought me, I couldn't eat that much. I did not have much of an appetite. I just wanted to be home with my family.

There was a routine to each day. Wake up at 7am then fold up the bed clothes that they had given you the night before. Sit and wait for the guards to open the huge steel door so you can put your things away in a little shelf. After you put your bedding away, you had time to brush your teeth and wash up a bit. This was done one cell at a time.

About every three days you had the opportunity to shave with an electric razor that everybody else was using, and showers were about once every four days. They did ask if you wanted to exercise, and if so, you were allowed to go to a large room to stretch and exercise as you desired.

I was amazed that it was orderly, quiet, and peaceful. There were no fights while I was there, and I was treated with dignity and respect.

You find in these situations what is most important to you, and I was glad that they allowed me to access my Bible for about nine hours each day. God's word sustained me and strengthened me as never before. I couldn't get enough of God's word each day.

One day as I was reading my Bible, Shrek tried to ask me what I did for a living. As I tried to communicate that I was a pastor, he understood that to be a teacher. He would point at my Bible and say, "Teacher?" and I would reply, "Yes." This told me that he must have had some understanding of Christianity or religion, whether from a good or bad example I did not know.

I could tell that Shrek was interested in my Bible, and in me. Donkey, however, was in another world. Shrek would try to say something to him about my Bible and that I was a teacher, and Donkey shrugged it off like he did not want to hear anything about it.

Of all the tattoos on his body, Shrek had one tattoo on his left forehand that was in English. In big, bold, capital letters he had tattooed on his hand: **LOVE**.

I was reading my Bible and I looked at Shrek and moved over to him to point at his hand and I pointed to my Bible and said, "God," and then I pointed to his hand and said, "loves you!"

Shrek looked at me with a bit of a smile and then looked up, put his hands together and acted as if to pray. I felt like God used that. I felt like the Holy Spirit was working in Shrek's life.

In the midst of my longing to be home and facing the humiliation of what I was going through, God had a plan for me to reveal His love to these men in the cell I was in. Is this why I was arrested? Was that God's purpose for me in this cell? How could I communicate the love of God to these men? I asked God to help me get through this ordeal, and help me communicate His love to these men. God was doing a work in my heart through Shrek and Donkey.

Donkey reminded me that Shrek was a former Japanese Mafia member. I'm not sure if he wanted to scare me, or what his intention was in telling me this. It's amazing how we size people up and determine they are either our friend or our enemy simply from appearances. God's love causes you to react in spiritual ways and not in the normal ways of our natural mindset.

On my fifth day, Donkey was released, and two other men joined Shrek and myself.

As I was trying to deal with the whole concept of being in jail, my mind would race to issues back home. One situation that was weighing heavily on my mind was our church facility. It is a long story, but at this time our church was in a very difficult place. Our facility was actually going through a foreclosure process that was no fault of our own. A public sale date was to be set, and there was a real possibility that while I was in jail, our facility would be sold and we would be homeless as a body of believers.

My wife and I are the only paid staff, so there was a lot of responsibility on my shoulders to steer us through these waters, but if I was not there, I was not quite sure what would happen. My heart was heavy for our congregation who had prayed, given, and supported the ministry for several years. To lose the facility would be tragic.

It was during these twelve days I sought God through prayer and His word, and He began to speak to me about several things in my life, ministry, and about the Christian walk.

As I have already said, this was the most difficult time of my life, but God had a plan. I was experiencing nights of discouragement like I had never experienced before. In the midst of it all, God brought peace and a knowledge that He was in control. I had a sense that God was going to turn everything around for my good, but I simply did not know how long it would take. Waiting is the hardest part. The faith to believe is one thing, but faith in the middle of the storm is the tough spot.

It is in moments and times like this when God refines, convicts, corrects, and develops us more into His image if we will listen to Him. I would never want to go through this experience again, but I know that I am better for it.

What was happening in my life was impacting literally hundreds, if not thousands, of other people.

My prayer is that these next chapters will encourage you in your faith and strengthen you. You might be going through a time this very moment that pushes you to your limit. It could be that you find yourself in what looks like a lose-lose situation. But God is your source of life and strength. God is working when you feel like nothing is happening. Don't judge things in the natural. Stand on God's word that He does not sleep or slumber. He's got you covered!

I'm not a seasoned author by any standards. The words that follow are from a genuine desire to give God all the credit He deserves for all that He taught me during this time, and for how He kept watch over me and my family. At times I was frightened or desperate, and at other times, I was losing my hope.

Proverbs 13:12 (NKJV) says, "Hope deferred makes the heart sick, but a longing fulfilled is a tree of life."

I was heart sick as I sat day after day in that jail, not knowing whether I would be released or if I would be sent somewhere else. My heart ached when I would think of my wife and what she must be going through, as well as my children. Probably the most difficult thought was what this was doing to my mother and my mother-in-law, as they are both up in years.

In my desperation and fleeting hope, I experienced first-hand that my brokenness was a doorway for the power of Christ to be revealed. When you are losing hope, please know that God is at work rebuilding, restoring, and redeeming. Always remember that while we are waiting for a prayer to be answered, God is always working for our good and for His glory.

One of the scriptures that became life to me is found in Psalm 121. Listen to this Psalm and let it encourage you right where you are.

Psalm 121:1 - 8

> 1 I lift up my eyes to the mountains – where does my help come from?
> 2 *My help comes from the **Lord***, the Maker of heaven and earth.
> 3 He will not let your foot slip – *he who watches over you **will not slumber***;
> 4 indeed, he who watches over Israel will **neither slumber nor sleep**.
> 5 *The Lord watches over **YOU*** – the Lord is your shade at your right hand;
> 6 the sun will not harm you by day, nor the moon by night.
> 7 *The Lord will **keep you** from all harm – **he will watch over your life***;
> 8 the Lord will watch over your coming and going both now and for evermore.

Our God doesn't go to sleep on the job! He's always watching out for us, and He's always working things out for our good. When you pray, it's not about getting what you want. Your prayer life should position you to get God what He wants.

I better try to wrap this chapter up!

My oldest son, Jevan, plays drums for our worship team and works with our youth. One of the responsibilities he has in our weekly services is to give announcements and updates. Every time he takes the microphone he always says this first: "Don't forget that God is good, all the time. And all the time, God is good."

That was a lifeline to me. It isn't just a cute little saying to pop off, but it is truth. God is good all the time, and all the time God is good.

Have you ever been afraid of the dark? Do you have memories as a child where your older siblings or friends would wait until it was dark to scare the living daylights out of you? Are you going through a situation right now where it seems that hope is lost, and that there is no way out?

I think the enemy of our soul likes to work most diligently at night and in the cover of dark.

It was as evening approached that hope would slip from my heart. Faith would be high throughout the day because I saw people coming and going. There was activity. Interviews were taking place, and lawyers would come in and out, so I thought as long as I saw activity there was hope that this would be my day to be released.

Then as late afternoon turned into early evening, my hopes were dashed and discouragement brought on by disappointment would weigh heavy on me.

When I could see that my release was not taking place, I would look forward to the evening routine because I just wanted to go to sleep so morning would come again, and with morning came a renewed hope that this might be the day deliverance came. Hope deferred was making my heart sick. Not being able to talk with my wife and kids was difficult, and I knew their hope was being tested as well.

Once again, it was God's word that would strengthen me and create hope inside of my heart.

I remembered reading John 16:33 (NIV) when Jesus was speaking to the disciples and reminded them, "I have told you these things, so that in me you may have peace. In this world you will have trouble. But take heart! I have overcome the world."

I had to remind myself that even though my circumstance was real, the fact that Jesus overcame death, hell, and the grave for me was even more real. I would overcome the fear by allowing the peace of Christ to reign in my heart and mind. I had to make a choice to believe God's word over the doubt and fear that was trying to rule my heart and mind.

Nights of discouragement were real, tangible, and if I let them they would have sucked the life completely from me. Discouragement does breed hopelessness, which gives birth to all kinds of negative actions, lifestyles, and addictions.

When I wondered how my family was doing, I was encouraged by the writings of the prophet Isaiah.

Isaiah 61:3 (NIV) says, "and provide for those who grieve in Zion to bestow on them a crown of beauty instead of ashes, the oil of joy instead of mourning, and a garment of praise instead of a spirit of despair. They will be called oaks of righteousness, a planting of the Lord for the display of his splendor."

Praise began to rise up inside of me and I would begin to praise God and thank Him because He was taking care of my family. I would praise Him because I knew that friends around the world were praying and interceding for me. I just knew it.

As I began to praise Him, the fear, despair, and hopelessness had no room to reside in my life. Despair was replaced with joy that God was doing something that was miraculous. I couldn't see it with my natural eyes, but in my spirit I had an unshakeable confidence that God was at work and I needed to somehow have patience for His plan to be fulfilled.

I began to thank God that He allowed me to experience this situation to develop areas of my life that were lacking or not even present at the time. I could praise Him because this situation was not a surprise to Him, so I could trust in His purpose and plan for me, my wife, my kids, my friends, my church, and the list goes on.

You need to develop your praise life now, because you will face events in your future that will require a deep praise to get you through it. Praise doesn't just happen. You must train yourself to praise God. You must instruct your heart and mind to praise God.

Too many people think that praise and worship is the responsibility of the worship team on Sunday's. No, no, no!

Praise is a weapon given to us by God to war against and to defeat the enemy. You can't reserve praise to the "song service." Praise must be a part of your daily lifestyle as much as reading God's word is. The truth is that praise and worship are directly attached to your prayer life.

You see, an apple tree produces apples just like an orange tree produces oranges. So it is with prayer and praise. If a believer doesn't demonstrate a lifestyle of praise in their life, I can guarantee you that prayer is absent from their life. They are inextricably connected.

Praise destroys hopelessness. Praise lifts your sights higher. Praise is a weapon that is essential to the life of every believer. Praise has nothing to do with vocal ability but everything to do with your knowledge of who God is and your relationship with Him.

Lights Out

On a comical note, I told you that when night would come I would desire to go to sleep quickly and wake to a hope that I could possibly be released the next day. It seemed that almost every night I wanted to go to sleep quickly, Shrek would want to communicate about American food or American movies. At first it would frustrate me because I didn't want to talk about any of those things. I just wanted to go home! However, God was using these simple conversations to help me build a relationship with Shrek. You see, nothing is wasted with God.

These conversations would turn into open doors to try and communicate Jesus' love to Shrek and the others in the cell with me. The Lord would also use these conversations about McDonald's, Terminator, and Rocky to give me perspective and lighten the heaviness. I would find myself laughing at times in the dark because of the simplicity of the communication, but the deep purpose in the meaning.

I'll give one last scripture for this chapter that I hope encourages you. There are many times in my life that I have said, "If it had not been for the Lord," and you can fill in the blank.

Psalm 124:2-5 (NIV) says that if "the Lord had not been on our side when people attacked us, they would have swallowed us alive when their anger flared against us; the flood would have engulfed us, the torrent would have swept over us, the raging waters would have swept us away."

If it had not been for the Lord, I would have lost my mind in that cell. I'm thankful to know on a personal level the God who created the universe. I'm grateful that He desires to know me, and He desires to have personal relationship with you as well.

May your nights of discouragement be washed away in the amazing love and grace of our Lord and Savior, Jesus Christ.

Chapter 4

Don't Doubt In The Dark What You Know To Be True In The Light

I spent that first night barely sleeping. To be honest, I didn't know if it was safe to go to sleep because of the other men in the cell with me. It was nerve wracking, but eventually I did find a few hours to rest.

As I woke up in jail for the first time in my life, the sign of daylight was a sign to me that there was hope for my release. It was a new day. Surely they will understand it was just a terrible mistake on my part, and they will release me.

As the lights came on in the jail, I was instructed to fold up my bedding and put it away neatly, then everyone had a responsibility to sweep the cell, mop the cell, and clean the toilet. This was a daily routine that helped to move the day along. After we would clean our cell, we were released in groups of 2 - 3 to wash and brush our teeth, then return to our cell and wait for breakfast to be served. I could shave only on certain days, and I was offered time outside of my cell about every other day to exercise in a secure area with one other person.

I wasn't really trying to get into shape, but if you're going to offer me an opportunity to get out of this cell then

I'm going to take it. I would basically use this time to walk and pray.

Once breakfast was over, you would begin to see men being taken to court or to speak with their lawyer, and then you had the opportunity to pick out reading materials. Thankfully, they allowed me to have my Bible and some other reading materials I had brought with me on the trip. This was a lifeline for me!

God spoke to me about various areas of my life and my relationship with Him as I devoured God's Word like a baby Christian. I was desperate to hear Him speak, and I found a new love for the Bible that I had taken for granted so many times.

It was usually during my reading time that a small army of police officers would march in with a chant and line up outside my cell. The first time it took me by surprise and I just wasn't sure what was about to take place.

They would instruct everyone to spread their hands and feet and lean against the wall as the officers searched the cell. Once they searched the cell they would begin their body search and a search of my reading materials. This process was foreign to me, and was quite stressful.

U.S. Consul Arrives

On the afternoon of Tuesday, April 12, I was informed that the U.S. Consul was here to see me. You have no idea how excited I was. I thought, "This is my ticket out of here! I am an American, and help is on the way! Strike up the National Anthem and wave Old Glory, because I'm going home!"

They put handcuffs on me and led me to a small little room where a middle-aged white woman and a Japanese woman were sitting on the other side of a glass wall. Neither of them smiled at me. They were all business. Their appearance gave no indication that they could help me, or that they even wanted to help me.

The U.S. Consul began by telling me that she could not help me. It was clear that I was under the laws and jurisdiction of the Japanese legal system, and the United States could not get involved. I broke a Japanese law, and I would have to face the Japanese judicial system.

She asked me for the names of people I would like her to contact to let them know where I was, and what had happened. That's all she said she could do.

I was provided with documents that would help me understand my charges and help prepare me for my stay. This was not a good meeting at all.

Then she dropped the bomb on me. The U.S. Consul informed me that I should prepare my mind to be in a Japanese prison for a long, long time. The charges against me carried a five-year prison sentence along with a $20,000 fine.

I began to provide her with the names and phone numbers of the people I would like her to contact so she could tell them my predicament. I gave her all the names I could think of, and especially asked her to contact my son who works for the U.S. State Department, and tell him to call my Nebraska Congressman right away so they would know where I am. Fear started to set in, and I just wanted somebody to know where I was.

The news got even worse. I was informed that in the Japanese court system, 99% of the cases that go to trial get convictions. Without God's help, there was really no way I was going home soon.

That was the first and the last time I saw the U.S. Consul.

I left that meeting depressed. I felt I was without hope, and if my country could not help me, I was in deep trouble. It's extremely hard to describe how this impacted me emotionally, spiritually, and mentally. Embarrassment was real. There was a real sense of failure. It started to get dark in my mind. I just couldn't believe this was happening to me. This was like the worst nightmare I could imagine.

It was at this point that as I sat in my cell that I began to write down a multitude of negative thoughts. This was a dark time for me. I was thinking the worst, and yet the peace of God began to wipe it away. As I began to write down two pages of negative thoughts of myself, it was here that I began to hear God's voice clearly.

I heard Him say, "I know the plans I have for you. Plans to prosper you, and not to harm you. Plans to give you a hope and a future."

God was trying to let me know that He had a perfect plan for my life, and that His plans would be fulfilled no matter how dark and desperate things might seem. His voice was the greatest lifeline and source of strength I could hold onto.

We have to understand that there is a real enemy of our soul, and his goal is to steal, kill, and destroy our future and our very lives. The enemy wants to start in our mind to create fear, doubt, and unbelief. If we begin to doubt, then our faith dwindles. If we begin to fall for the tactics of fear, then we find ourselves vulnerable to his assault. My mind was under attack, and the battle was fierce for me to hold onto the truth of God's Word.

If Satan can discourage us to the point at which we lose hope, we then stop living out our God-given purpose. Dr. Myles Monroe used to say, "The graveyard is filled with glory unrevealed."

What he was saying was that because of fear and hopeless-ness, people stop living out the purpose and plan of God for themselves, and they end up going to the grave with an unfinished life.

That's why it is important to feed your mind every day with the word of God. God's word will literally transform your mind from hopelessness to having a reason for waking up every morning. The word of God is powerful and will give you the grace to move forward in life.

When you feed your mind and spirit with God's Word, you will find strength and hope in the midst of every situation that challenges your life. The truth of God's word defeats the enemy's attempts to steal, kill, and destroy.

It was at this point that I began to be thankful for being raised in a faith-filled, Bible teaching church because I began to alter my thoughts and grab on to what I really knew to be truth from God's word that I had experienced throughout my upbringing.

You see, when you are faced with temptation or stressful life experiences, whatever is inside of you is what will come out of you. I'm not at all saying I had this under control, but what I am saying is that because the word of God was planted in my life, it brought a harvest of faith and trust that God was in control even when it appeared life was out of control.

Shrek and Donkey must have thought I was a crazy man. I'm sure they had never seen a crazy American like me before! I began to walk and pace around in the cell speaking these words out loud, "Jeff, don't doubt in the dark what you know to be true in the light! Jeff, you know that God is good!"

Then I would say, "Jeff, don't doubt in the dark what you know to be true in the light! God loves you, and will never abandon you!"

I did this for the longest time, and it seemed that every time I would declare these truths out loud that my faith would get stronger. Fear would disappear. I would have confidence that God was taking care of my family, and hope began to rise in my heart.

Here are some of the other declarations that I made. If you are going through a challenging circumstance right now, I want to encourage you to insert your name and begin to make these declarations out loud, and I believe you'll experience the same thing I did.

Don't doubt in the dark what you know to be true in the light:

- God is good all the time!
- God is for me!
- God deserves my praise right now!

- God is faithful and true!
- No weapon formed against me will prosper!
- God hears me!
- I am loved by God!
- God never fails!
- God will answer me!
- All things work together for the good of those who love God and are called according to His purpose!
- My steps are ordered of the Lord!
- God is watching over my family!
- God has not given me a spirit of fear, but of power, love, and a sound mind!
- God is Jehovah-Shammah, The God who is there!
- God is Jehovah-Jireh, my Provider!
- He is Jehovah-Elyon, The Most High God!
- He is Jehovah-El Shaddai, The Lord God Almighty / All Sufficient One!
- He is Jehovah Rohi, The Good Shepherd!
- Psalm 23, The Lord is my shepherd, I want for nothing!
- He is Jehovah Nissi, My Banner & Victory!
- God's ways are higher and His thoughts are higher!

Truth is not determined by our situation or circumstance. Truth is rock solid and it never changes. Truth will withstand each and every storm of our lives.

If you want to know the truth, then you need to know the person of Jesus Christ. Jesus is the way, the *truth*, and the life! Don't fall for lies. You can walk in the truth when you put your faith and trust in Jesus Christ.

I only had that one dark day of discouragement, because I made a decision to believe the truth despite my surroundings. My thoughts were raised higher when I began to declare the truth of who God is and who I am in Him. It was when I chose to align my mind with the mind of Christ that my burdens were being lifted. My view of my situation changed as I praised God. My view of those in the cell with me changed, and my view of those who had charged me changed.

Praise does not always remove you from a situation, but it will reveal God's power in your situation as you align your thoughts on Him.

Maybe you are in a difficult situation right now. It might seem like there is no way out. Start to declare who God is. Open your mouth and declare who you are in Him, and watch what happens. You are God's beloved!

You see, God is always asking us to come up higher to where He is.

Chapter 5

The Prosecutor, The Judge, and My Attorney

O n day three I started my day with the same routine. I followed all the instructions about putting my bedding away, cleaning the cell, washing up and brushing my teeth, and waiting for breakfast to come.

Shortly after breakfast the jailer came to my cell and held a book up for me to read. On one side of the page it had instructions in Japanese and on the other side it was in English. He pointed to a statement that said I was going for an interview with the prosecutor.

This was terribly stressful as they escorted me out of the cell into a small room where they were meticulous in searching me and preparing me for transfer. I was handcuffed and led by several officers through the facility outside to a waiting van where there was an army of officers surrounding the parking lot just in case someone decided to make their big break.

By day three I was glad to go anywhere just to get some fresh air and see more than the inside of a jail cell.

As we made the 20–25 minute journey to the courthouse, I tried to see if I could remember the area we were in, but it was not familiar. Once we pulled up to the courthouse,

I was quickly taken inside and put on an elevator with my nose in the corner until we got to the holding area.

I was taken to a cell with other inmates where prisoners are held until the prosecutor is ready to see them. I quietly prayed the whole time I was in the holding cell.

They eventually led me out of the cell and down a hallway into a small room where I was seated across from the prosecutor and handcuffed to the chair. There was a court reporter and a translator with us as well, but no representation for me.

The Translator read the police report of the events that led to my arrest, and then read the charges I was facing. After she read this information, I was asked to make a statement.

I looked the prosecutor in the eyes and apologized for offending her and her nation in such a way as I did. I assured her that it was a terrible oversight on my part in packing, and that I would never intentionally bring a weapon, ammunition, or anything of the sort with me to a foreign country.

I explained that I have visited Okinawa for many years, and would never want to jeopardize the opportunity to enter her nation. Finally, I simply humbled myself and asked for mercy in this matter.

The prosecutor was not impressed. She looked me squarely in the eyes and informed me that they would have to do a full investigation because she didn't know if I was buying arms, selling arms, or if I might be a terrorist. Those were the words she used with me.

She was firm when she informed me that the Japanese do not tolerate weapons or drugs in the country. According to the prosecutor, the only people who have weapons in Japan are the police and the Japanese Mafia. This was not going well.

I was once again asked to sign some documents, then the officers took me back to the holding cell to wait for the other inmates to be heard by the prosecutor, after which we would all return to the detention center.

Two days later, I went through the whole process again of being transported to another location to meet with the judge who was even sterner than the prosecutor. My visit with the judge lasted about three whole minutes. He basically let me know that I was guilty because I confessed that the bullet was mine. He didn't show any mercy with me and asked me to leave his office.

God Has A Plan

When I returned from the prosecutor's office, I was pretty discouraged. It's funny now, but Shrek could tell I was a little down and he was making his best effort to encourage me.

Later that day I was asked to come to the cell door and the jailer informed me that my appointed attorney was here to see me. He asked me if I wanted to speak with the attorney, and I told him that I did.

They escorted me to a small room, and when they opened the door I was surprised to recognize the individual who would be my attorney sitting on the other side of the glass. A woman was smiling at me, and before I even got into the room I asked, "What are you doing here?" She lifted her hands high, and said, "I'm your attorney!"

I had met Annette Callagain at the Great Co-Mission Conference with Bishop Whitaker, but I didn't know she was an attorney. She told me that she actually felt like the Lord wanted her to give me her business card on Sunday, but she just didn't do it.

Well, I was happy to see a familiar face, and even happier to find out she was a pretty good attorney. This was something only God could set up. Ms. Callagain is the only attorney in Okinawa who can practice both Japanese and Nebraska law. You have to see that God was aware of this and had a divine plan because only God could arrange this. Some 20 years ago, Annette actually taught at Central High School in Omaha, which is only five minutes from the church that I pastor! Talk about a set up by God!

This was encouraging to me. My faith began to rise inside as I realized how God had been aligning this moment not just at that time but also literally for many years prior.

This one moment gave me so much hope. It showed me the detail and the precision by which God operates. It was undeniable that something much larger was taking place in our lives.

At one point, I broke down in tears, partly because I was amazed by God and partly because the whole experience of being in jail, facing the prosecutor and judge, the searches, and all that was involved in being in jail was just overwhelming to me.

Annette and I had a great visit, and she assured me that she would keep my wife up to date on the process of my case. She allowed me to give her some specific words to share with my wife and my kids. It was such a blessing to know that Annette would be able to communicate with my family. My main concern was to let my wife and kids know that I was okay, and that I was being treated well. I just didn't want them to worry.

Our meeting concluded, and Annette got to work right away. She brought on to her team a man by the name of Takaesu-Sensei, who had once been the District Attorney in Okinawa. This meant that he had access to the prosecutor at just about any time he would like. Man, at this point I felt like God blessed me with the Dream Team!

Annette assured me that everything was going to work out. She explained that there was a process, and we just had to let the process take its course.

The Process

You know, God has a process in our lives too. We don't like difficult situations. None of us wants to face adversity. However, it's often through adversity that God's purposes are revealed. In adversity we see the power of God's word manifested.

The ultimate scene of adversity took place on a hill called Calvary. The disciples could not see the death of Jesus as the plan they had dreamed of. In their minds, they were all thinking that it was over, but God's process was fully in place and at work on their behalf. As a matter of fact, God's process at Calvary was for the entire world's benefit.

You see, in order to have a resurrection, there must be a death.

Your dream might appear to be dying right now. It might look in the natural like it's over. It's finished. But it's all connected to the process of God.

Sometimes dreams have to die in order for the dream God has for our lives to be fulfilled.

I want to encourage you. The prosecutor and the judge might have handed down your sentence, but don't forget you have an undefeated defense attorney whose name is Jesus. And until He speaks, it's not over!

Chapter 6

Going Home

The way the Japanese legal system works is that they have an immediate three days to hold an individual that has been arrested for potentially committing a crime. After the three days the prosecutor has an opportunity to ask the judge for more time to investigate the situation, and ultimately they have 13 days to hold you. After the 13 days are up, they have to let you go if they are not going to take your case to court.

Just a little encouraging information the U.S. Consul wanted me to be aware of was that 99% of ALL cases that go to court are convictions. Basically, if they take you to court, you are going to prison for however long they determine. Obviously, this was a concern to me.

However, on day 10 I kind of got the idea something was changing for me. I was taken to the prosecutor's office again for another "interview."

On the ride over to the courthouse, the van driver and four other police officers initiated conversation with me. The police officer closest to me began pointing out the Japanese Naval Base as we passed by, and other landmarks in the city. Somehow we got into a conversation about sports, and he had played some baseball in his youth. He made mention that one of the other police officers was some kind of martial arts expert. Their conversation with me was filled with laughter, and it was light-hearted, which had never taken place in our previous encounters.

We went through the same routine of exiting the vehicle and being rushed down a hallway to the elevator and on up to the holding cell until the prosecutor was ready to see me. I didn't have to wait long, and it was time to see her again.

It appeared to me when I sat down before the prosecutor that her demeanor had drastically changed toward me. She asked me the same questions from our original interview, but when I would answer her she would respond with a merciful response, confirming what I had just said. In other words, she was almost helping me craft my statement.

As the interview began to wind down, she didn't tell me I was going to be released but she did say that the next time I visit Okinawa, I should be more careful packing my bags. At this point, she said the interview was over and I was returned to the jail.

At the jail, I had a visit from Bishop Whitaker who had returned from his medical mission to the Philippines. In our conversation, he said he thought he should go to the airport and pick up my checked bags that had been left there from my original flight. When Bishop got there, the police had beaten him to it and had the luggage back at the jail where I was being held.

Later in the evening I was asked by the police to come to an interview room, and they had my checked luggage there. In a room probably seven feet by seven feet were several police officers and myself. It was crowded, and they wanted me to open my checked bags so they could examine them.

I have to be honest. I was scared. Was there another bullet in my checked bags? Did they plant something in my bags? I began to sweat a little bit, and then I just took a deep breath and opened it up and trusted Jesus.

To my surprise, they had me open it but quickly said close it up. They didn't even examine the entire bag or pockets. We zipped it up and they put tape over the zipper and had me sign it. They told me they would keep it here at the jail until I was released.

The next morning I went through the same routine, and then after lunch a police officer came to my cell door and asked me to come read the book he held up. He pointed to this statement:

Your papers have been signed, and you are released.

I couldn't believe what I was reading! I got excited and started to cry all at the same time. Shrek was seated to my right, and when I turned around and saw him I started crying like a baby. It was the strangest feeling, and I can't explain it other than I wanted so bad to know for sure that He knew Jesus. The other feeling I had was that of being grateful because Shrek had kind of looked out for me over the past twelve days. I grabbed Shrek's hand and just said, "Thank you!"

They don't waste time when it's your time to be released. As soon as I read the book, the door opened, and they rushed me to an interview room and begin returning to me my personal belongings.

I remember telling the detectives as they led me down the hallway to meet Bishop Whitaker that I was sorry that I wasted their time over these days because of a careless act on my part.

When I saw Bishop Whitaker I got pretty happy. It just seemed surreal that this had all just happened to me, and now I was actually being released. They released me without having to pay any monetary fine as well. That was a total miracle!

My first phone call was in the car to my wife. I can't explain how it felt to hear her voice and tell her how much I loved her. That was the best phone call I've ever had. I was able to say these words to the love of my life: "I'm coming home!"

Bishop Whitaker and I embraced, and the same detectives who had interrogated me walked us out of the jail, and man did that feel good!

We got in Bishop's car and went to eat lunch together, and to see if my airline ticket was still good. Because I was arrested at the airport, my original airline ticket was voided and we needed to purchase another ticket.

I spent the night in Okinawa, and on April 23, 2016, I boarded my flight to the United States to be reunited with my family.

I hope that you will continue reading this book, because the reason for this book lies in the pages to come. The events of these twelve days spent in a Japanese jail contained purpose, correction, instruction, and rebuke from the Lord. If we don't learn from our past, we will certainly repeat the it.

May the lessons I learned and will discuss in the upcoming pages of this book speak to your life and draw you closer to God.

Chapter 7

The Cost Of Carelessness

On Monday, April 11, I was arrested at Naha International Airport for the violation of arms and swords laws of Japan because airport officials found one round of 9mm ammunition in my carry-on bag. It seemed harmless and insignificant. However, to the Japanese it was a very serious offense.

This chapter is probably the most important chapter of the book, because the most important lesson I learned from this experience was the *cost of my carelessness*. God spoke to me clearly over these days in jail about how what we think is the smallest thing can be the biggest and most destructive issue in our lives.

It became abundantly clear to me over those twelve days in jail that what I considered to be harmless, insignificant, and no big deal actually was a big deal to God. The things that I assumed God overlooked turned out to be very offensive to Him.

One careless oversight on my part in packing my luggage ended up costing me twelve days in jail. It caused my family an extreme amount of stress and worry, and our future was literally in question. My careless act could have been avoided if I had been careful in packing my bags. I would have seen it if I hadn't been in such a hurry, and I most definitely would have removed that one bullet.

I simply never saw it because I didn't examine my bag thoroughly. All my books and materials for my trip were packed tightly into my carry-on bag, and I simply didn't take the time to make sure it was completely cleaned out of other items that I had previously carried in that bag. Unnecessary items for this trip should have been removed.

Psalm 139:23 (KJV) says, "Search me, O God, and know my heart: try me, and know my thoughts."

As a follower of Jesus, it is imperative that we take the time to inspect our lives to make sure that we are clean of anything that could cause us to stray from the faith or dilute our testimony for Christ. Inviting our heavenly Father to search our heart is wisdom. We have blind spots and we need the Father's perspective to reveal things that might be hidden from our view, just like this one round of ammunition was hidden from my view.

People are watching our lives. They don't just listen to what we say, but they examine our actions with our wife, our kids, our ministry, and every aspect of our daily lives. What we think is no big deal can be a deal breaker for someone who is contemplating serving the Jesus that we serve.

It seems that few people enjoy examinations or tests of any kind; however, scripture reminds us that we need to have periodic examinations to confirm we are still in the faith. There is a risk that if you are careless with your faith you could fail the test in the end.

There was a passage of scripture that just jumped out at me throughout this situation. This scripture spoke to me of what I had done, but more importantly how careless I can be with my walk of faith.

This passage of scripture from the Apostle Paul is proof that it is possible to fail the test of faith.

2 Corinthians 13:5 (NIV) says, "Examine yourselves to see whether you are in the faith; test yourselves. Do you not realize that Christ Jesus is in you—*unless, of course, you fail the test*?"

Notice Paul didn't mention religion. He didn't mention church membership. Paul implores us to examine ourselves to see if we are *in the faith*. It's like getting ready to take an exam in school when you test yourself the night before the real test to make sure you know what you need to know to pass the test.

When was the last time you examined yourself? Do you remember the last time that you were really honest about your relationship with Jesus? Could it be that if you don't examine yourself you could get off course?

As a pastor I see it all the time. People neglect to remain disciplined in their relationship with the Father and end up taking their faith for granted. Compromise sets in. Things that used to convict them are now common practices in their lives.

The writer of Hebrews speaks to us in Chapter 2 and verse 1,

"Therefore we must pay much closer attention to what we have heard, lest we *drift away* from it."

I've seen many people throughout my life that started out strong for Jesus, but then they allowed things to slip into their lives. A compromise here and a compromise there led to bigger compromises that ended up leading them to drift away from their relationship with Jesus.

The foundational truths of the Word of God must not be compromised, and the daily disciplines of keeping our relationship with Jesus exciting must be a priority, or we could ultimately drift away and fail the test.

Our enemy enjoys luring us with small but subtle areas of compromise. We can be "doing" all the things that appear to make one a Christian, yet we stop "being" the new creation that scripture reveals we are. One small area of hidden sin that is left unattended will open the door for destruction if it is not surrendered at the foot of the cross to Jesus.

The Israelites had no problem destroying Jericho because they trusted in God and they obeyed His instructions. Jericho was a fortified city that in the natural could not be destroyed. However, when we follow God's instructions, the impossible is made possible. The natural is overwhelmed by the supernatural of God.

The problem with the Israelites lay with one man's disobedience to God's instructions at Jericho. Achan decided that God was not talking to him when he decided to take some of the devoted things for himself. His one, unnoticed act of disobedience caused the Israelites to get routed by a tiny little army from Ai. Not only did many Israelites die in this battle that they had to retreat from but also Achan along with all of his family lost their lives because of what seemed to be a small, insignificant, hidden act of disobedience that God was fully aware of.

I would speak to all of my ministry friends. At times we are doing everything on the outside that looks like we're close to Jesus. We can do ministry blindfolded, so to speak. By everyone's measure we are on our way to heaven with multiplied rewards awaiting us. Yet Jesus said that we could be fooling ourselves if we were not careful.

Matthew 7:21–23 (NIV) "Not everyone who says to me, 'Lord, Lord,' will enter the kingdom of heaven, but only the one who does the will of my Father who is in heaven. Many will say to me on that day, 'Lord, Lord, did we not prophesy in your name and in your name drive out demons and in your name perform many miracles?' Then I will tell them plainly, 'I never knew you. Away from me, you evildoers!'"

I never knew you! None of us want to hear that from Jesus. Yet if we don't take closer examinations of our lives from time to time, we could find ourselves being labeled an 'evildoer' by Jesus.

Nobody wants to fail. However, without periodic examination in our lives, there is a real possibility that we could fail and miss out on what God desires us to experience for all eternity. This scripture was ringing loud and clear to me while I was sitting and contemplating how I got into this situation.

No matter how culture shifts and changes, our God does not change. His path is still a narrow road. God's standard continues to stand the test of time. Though our laws change and definitions change, we serve a God whose principles remain the same throughout all of time.

A few years ago I had the opportunity to visit Cuba, and one of the national leaders was sharing with me how God had poured His Spirit out on Cuba and a mighty revival broke out. This man's office was small, and had a very narrow doorway to enter through. Now, this man was short and—forgive me—he was pretty wide. He actually had to turn sideways to get through the door into his office.

I asked him why the door was so narrow, and he smiled and leaned in to say, 'Because it reminds me every time I come to my office that the road is narrow to heaven.'

Wow! What a reminder for us today. If we would examine ourselves we would find out what pleases or displeases the Father, and we would be prepared for eternity.

The cost of carelessness is a high price that none of us wants to pay. This one small act of carelessness on my part impacted many people. My wife and children, along with all of my extended family were impacted by my oversight in packing. My church and leadership team were impacted.

I remember apologizing to the police officers and detectives for taking 12 days of their time and effort that could have been focused on something more important. My careless act impacted their lives as well.

Some of the areas God spoke to me about being careless are listed below. Maybe God is speaking to you about similar areas. I encourage you to do what I did. Simply repent and ask the Father for forgiveness, and grace to overcome. God is faithful to answer your prayer.

God's Word

God showed me that I took His written Word for granted. There were areas in my life for which I didn't look to God's word for direction, peace, and guidance. I had been careless in my handling of God's word. There were issues that I felt I could handle myself, so I didn't need to bother God with them.

Proverbs 3:5–6 (NKJV): "Lean not on your own understanding. In all your ways acknowledge him and he will direct your paths."

Matthew 5:6 (NKJV): "Blessed *are* those who hunger and thirst for righteousness, for they shall be filled."

I found myself being filled with things of this world that could never take the place of God's Word and righteousness in my life.

I was convicted that I had not continued to give God's Word the place of devotion and priority in my life that is needed on a daily basis.

His word guides us, corrects us, encourages us, and much more. The Word is alive. Psalm 119:11 (KJV) says, "Thy word have I hid in my heart that I might not sin against thee."

How many sins have crept into our lives because we have been careless to hide God's word in our heart? We could be spared a multitude of trouble if we would treat God's word with fresh respect and devotion.

In these last days we hear various new doctrines and teachings that lure people away from the truth, and it is

His Word that will keep us from falling prey to these false doctrines and teachings that would steal our faith. It seems if someone has apostle or prophet in front of their name, or they have their own television program that they must be anointed and called of God. Listen to what the prophet Micah had to say about this.

Micah 2:11 (NIV) says, "If a liar and deceiver comes and says, 'I will prophesy for you plenty of wine and beer, _he would be just the prophet for this people_.'"

You see, instead of testing the spirits and knowing God's word and voice for ourselves, we just go along with these new noisemakers. Carelessness to know God's word and His voice will cost you dearly!

I had been careless with my personal testimony. There is no one that can share my story and testimony like me. Our personal testimony is one of the best ways to lead people to Jesus.

The Lord revealed to me how I had been careless with my family and friends. It seems that if we are not careful we are the most careless with those who are closest to us and love us the most.

When I was a youth pastor I would tell teenagers, "You show me your friends, and I'll show you your future." Even as an adult, it is important that I evaluate my personal relationships and friendships. Not everyone is looking out for my success. I'm not talking about career and money specifically. I'm talking about my success as a man of God, and as a husband and father.

I have to be careful to recognize that not everyone wants me to succeed in advancing the Gospel of Jesus with the gifts, talents, and abilities and the call that is on my life.

The House of God

Many people have lost their commitment to the House of God. We come when we want and stay home because we're just tired or have some other excuse to spend our time on fleshly pleasure.

Psalm 92:13 (NIV) reminds us, "Those that be planted in the house of the LORD will flourish in the courts of our God."

Maybe the reason you seem to be dissatisfied with the gathering of believers you associate with is that you have lost your commitment to the House of God. It's easy to complain, but it's another thing to be all in and make a difference through serving, loving, and being accountable to others.

People are down on what they are not up on. If you're rarely around, there is no way you can be in full relationship with the family of God. In that light, it's easy to just complain and find fault.

How can you say you love God but you don't love or like His Church! That just doesn't make sense as a believer.

Remember this—the Church is the Bride of Christ. God loves His Church! He gave His Only Son for the redemption of His Bride, the Church! Get in and give yourself to the Body of Christ, and you'll find satisfaction and contentment.

The Lord went on to stress to me to examine myself in the way I handle my purpose, my finances as well as my talents and abilities. He even went on to speak to me about my health and how I am treating His Temple! If we're going to be effective for God to use us, we need to take care of our bodies so we can go the long haul for the King.

I came home with a new perspective on my walk with Jesus, and in almost every area of my life. There is a new appreciation for the little things that I've so often taken for granted.

Where have you been careless? What is God saying to you as you read this chapter?

I believe that we are living in the day and hour when Jesus could return to the earth. May I challenge you to not be careless with your time on this earth and the responsibility to make disciples of all nations? I would also like to challenge you to not be careless with your spouse and children.

Be encouraged to take time even now to examine yourself to see if you are in the faith. Humble yourself and listen to the voice of God. You know His voice, and I know that He is speaking to you right now because you are His beloved.

Chapter 8

Stand

saiah 7:9b (NIV): "If you do not stand firm in your faith, you will not stand at all."

Nothing exposes the foundation of your life more than a crisis. A crisis will reveal whether or not you will sink or swim.

Where do you turn when you're facing a challenge in life? What is your life built upon? If you don't know, you had better find out because a storm is coming that will tear your house down if you're not building on the right foundation.

Jesus tells the parable of the wise builder and the foolish builder in the Gospel of Matthew, Chapter 7. Jesus was talking about people who practice His teachings as opposed to those whose talk has no walk to it. In other words, coming to church doesn't make you a Christian any more than walking into McDonald's makes you a Big Mac!

Many people call themselves Christians but do not practice the teachings of Jesus. Jesus made it clear to all of us in John 14:15 when He said, "If you love Me, keep my commands." It's not optional! There's no negotiating here. If you love the Master, you'll follow the Master's instructions on how to live life despite what others think, say, believe, or don't believe.

I am far from a perfect individual, but I can tell you that I've trusted in Jesus since I was 8 years old. He fulfills all of His promises. There has never been a time when He failed me. I can say like King David in Psalm 37:25 (NIV), "Once I was young, and now I am old. I have never seen the righteous forsaken, nor their seed begging bread."

If you build your life on the solid foundation of Almighty God, you will stand every test and storm that life brings you.

Throughout my life I have experienced trials. As a child, I faced abandonment from my father. It was in this season as a young boy that God's word kept me from the storm of abandonment destroying my life through drug abuse, alcohol, or any other manifestation of a young boy who is crying out for help because he's hurting deep inside.

Though my earthly father walked out, my heavenly Father did not. I found God nearer to me as I trusted in Him and held onto His promises. I would stand on God's Word in Psalm 68:5 (NIV) that says that God is "a father to the fatherless, a defender of widows, is God in his holy dwelling."

It was evident to me that God was close to me, and that He was filling a hole in my heart that no one and nothing else could fill and bring healing to my life. Standing in my faith despite whatever storm was crashing down on my life has been my anchor.

I have faced betrayal, job loss, the loss of children through miscarriage, and much more. Through every storm of life, it has been God's word that has sustained me, strengthened me, and developed God's character in my life.

The Word of God has sustained me through every storm that I have faced as a boy, a man, a husband, a father, and grandfather. God is faithful to keep all of His promises! If He has done it for me, I know He will do it for you! He is no respecter of persons.

You don't want to get into a storm and find out you didn't build on a solid foundation. You had better build your life right, by making sure you are on a firm foundation. That firm foundation is the word of God, and Jesus Himself. He is the rock you are to build your life on.

Matthew 7:24–27 (NIV):

"Therefore everyone who hears these words of mine and puts them into practice is like a wise man who built his house on the rock. The rain came down, the streams rose, and the winds blew and beat against that house; yet it did not fall, because it had its foundation on the rock. But everyone who hears these words of mine and does not put them into practice is like a foolish man who built his house on sand. The rain came down, the streams rose, and the winds blew and beat against that house, and it fell with a great crash."

This storm that entered our lives on April 11th, 2016 was simply an opportunity for my foundation to be revealed. The storm didn't win. I won because my foundation didn't crumble with the shaking of the storm. The storm simply revealed my source of strength and life.

What are you building your life on? If the rain and winds of life are beating your house down, rebuild your life on a new foundation. Let Jesus be the cornerstone and foundation of your life. I'll close with these powerful words from the Apostle Paul to the Church of Ephesus.

Ephesians 6:13 (NIV):

Therefore put on the full armor of God, so that when the day of evil comes, you may be able to *stand your ground*, and after you have done everything, to *stand*.

The ultimate plan of God for your life is not to destroy you, but to help you stand during every test, every trial, and every attack of the enemy by His power.

If you will decide today to build your life on God's Word, you will have personal stories of God's grace to share with others who have yet to experience His power.

Chapter 9

The Struggle Is Real

Ephesians 6:12 (NIV): "For our struggle is not against flesh and blood, but against the rulers, against the authorities, against the powers of this dark world and against the spiritual forces of evil in the heavenly realms."

During my stay in the Japanese detention center, it didn't take long for me to realize that there was a real spiritual war going on in my life. Our ministry was in the middle of a difficult season when our building was in jeopardy, and we were seeking God for His plan to be revealed. The location of our ministry is strategic in our community, and the enemy doesn't like to give up turf that he has ruled for a long time without a real fight.

So while I was 10,000 miles away from home, sitting in a detention center, my thoughts were racing as to the real possibility that our building could be sold out from underneath us. The uncertainty of the future of our ministry was in question, and we needed a supernatural breakthrough to seal the deal.

Where would we move? Who would lead while I was away? Would the congregation stay unified if this lasted a long time?

These were some of the real questions that ran through my mind. Once again, there was much that was out of my control, I had to trust God with my life, my family, and my ministry.

While praying and reading through God's Word, I was reminded of Paul writing to the Ephesians about being ready for battle. I (we) were in a real battle that required focus, faith, and trust in God's plans.

You may know this scripture well, but I want you to see what the Apostle Paul was saying.

Ephesians 6:10–18 (NIV): "Finally, be strong in the Lord and in his mighty power. Put on the full armor of God, so that you can take your stand against the devil's schemes. For our struggle is not against flesh and blood, but against the rulers, against the authorities, against the powers of this dark world and against the spiritual forces of evil in the heavenly realms. Therefore put on the full armor of God, so that when the day of evil comes, you may be able to stand your ground, and after you have done everything, to stand. Stand firm then, with the belt of truth buckled around your waist, with the breastplate of righteousness in place, and with your feet fitted with the readiness that comes from the gospel of peace. In addition to all this, take up the shield of faith, with which you can extinguish all the flaming arrows of the evil one. Take the helmet of salvation and the sword of the Spirit, which is the word of God. And pray in the Spirit on all occasions with all kinds of prayers and requests. With this in mind, be alert and always keep on praying for all the Lord's people."

Paul encourages us to "be strong" in the Lord. He didn't say to pull ourselves up by the bootstraps, brush that dirt off, and get moving. He makes it clear that our strength comes from God and God alone. I could not find real strength in myself in a situation like this. I cannot find strength in my knowledge or anywhere else, but in my weakness I can experience the strength of God.

After the shock of being arrested, I had to come to terms with the fact that this was a spiritual battle I was facing. It was incumbent upon me to "change my clothes." I had to exchange my natural thinking for thoughts that were higher. It was necessary for me to put on the armor of God and get in the battle. This was not between me and the prosecutor or judge. This was a direct onslaught from the pit of hell for the purpose of God to advance.

The Lord made me aware that even as Paul was writing here to the Ephesians, there were schemes being activated by the enemy of my soul. These schemes could not be conquered by any means other than spiritual warfare. I began to pray in the Spirit and declare God's Word over my situation. As I sought the Lord in prayer, I sensed two specific schemes that the enemy was launching.

The first scheme that was being activated against me was the spirit of false accusation. In an earlier chapter I mentioned that I felt like the detectives were trying hard to wear me down and get me to say something that they could use for their case that simply wasn't true.

Not only were the detectives working hard but Satan was also working hard on my mind with accusations. Scripture reminds us that this is one of his personality characteristics. He is the accuser of the brethren. He throws false accusations at us to try to break our faith and trust in God. He attacks our mind, and this is the reason we must train our minds with the word of God so that we are transformed and renewed.

Revelation 12:10 (NKJV) says, "Then I heard a loud voice saying in heaven, 'Now salvation, and strength, and the kingdom of our God, and the power of His Christ have come, for the accuser of our brethren, who accused them before our God day and night, has been cast down.'"

His destiny is clear! Satan will be destroyed and ultimately cast down forevermore. This will be the end for Satan.

Just as our enemy has a destiny, so do you and I. We are destined for victory through the blood of Jesus Christ, our Lord! You and I are already positioned as over-comers, and it is our responsibility to live out what God has already decided in the here and now.

I took full responsibility for my careless act of not seeing a bullet in my carry-on bag; however, the bullet was just an avenue for the enemy to release a scheme of false accusation on my life.

The second scheme that I recognized was the spirit of pride. It was evident from the first time I sat in front of the prosecutor and every time I met with the detectives. There was a spirit of pride to convict me, even if on false terms.

Earlier I mentioned that 99% of all cases that go to trial in Japan end with conviction, and I felt like pride was driving individuals to make sure that happened in my case.

When the enemy launches schemes against your life, you will need to put on the spiritual armor that God has freely given you to defend yourself and to claim your victory. It might not be gained in one night of prayer, but it will be gained! The shield of faith and the sword of the Spirit were vital to my sanity and confidence in the Lord. Fiery darts of accusation were being launched my direction and it was my faith that was able to defend me from each one of them. Just like the detectives were trying to break me down and get me to confess to something more than carelessness, the enemy of our soul was trying to get me to give into false accusations and lies about my Heavenly Father.

Satan loves to use the difficult times in our life to try to say that God won't come through, and that prayer works for other people but not you. He tries to attack our mind with false accusations to wear us down and confuse us.

There is nothing more powerful than the word of God. As I would read God's Word and begin to declare it verbally, I was strengthened in my spirit to fight this battle. There was a true confidence that I had already obtained my victory, but with the knowledge that I must continue to launch my attack of God's word upon the enemy.

One of the most important verses I would quote, sing, and declare constantly is found in the book of Isaiah. Isaiah 54:17 NKJV says, No weapon formed against you shall prosper, and every tongue which rises against you in judgment You shall condemn. This is the heritage of the servants of the Lord, and their righteousness is from Me," says the Lord.

I would put on my Fred Hammond voice and go to worshiping and declaring this scripture over and over again. As I would sing it, I would feel God's presence and peace overwhelm me. What a weapon to have at your disposal! Simply to know that because I am a child of the Most High God I have already won! This was essential to my perseverance.

Even though I was still locked up, my confidence was strong, knowing that it didn't matter what the enemy threw my way, that I was already victorious. It didn't matter what words of accusation the enemy would launch at me, the accusation was shot down before it ever reached the ears of my heart.

As you face your tests and your trials, you need to know that God saw it coming before it ever came to reality in your life. You too can stand confident that no weapon designed to destroy you can prosper! But you also need to arm yourself with God's armor to recognize the attack for what it is, and open your mouth to proclaim God's Word with authority and faith to see your victory through.

In the days that I spent in jail I was able to read nearly 80% of the Bible. The word of God was more my desire than any natural food that they would bring me. The proof of that is the fact that I almost read the entire Word in those twelve days, and the fact that I literally lost 20 pounds!

One of the things I am grateful for is that my mother put me in situations as a young boy to appreciate the power of God's Word. We need to position our children to hear, experience, and see the power of God's word in their lives so that as they will desire it for their entire lives.

I could not get enough of it! I kept reading, and reading, and God kept speaking to me.

From The First Day

Another passage of scripture that was significant to me was found in the book of Daniel, Chapter 10. It is here that Daniel is fasting and seeking God for twenty-one days, and he experiences a vision with an angel speaking to him. It reads,

Daniel 10:12– 14 (NIV): "Then he continued, 'Do not be afraid, Daniel. *Since the first day that you set your mind to gain understanding and to humble yourself before your God, your words were heard, and I have come in response to them.* But the prince of the Persian kingdom resisted me twenty-one days. Then Michael, one of the chief princes, came to help me, because I was detained there with the king of Persia. Now I have come to explain to you what will happen to your people in the future, for the vision concerns a time yet to come.'"

When I read this, my faith just increased when I read that "since the first day….your words were heard, and I have come in response to them." I felt like I could rip the cell doors open at this point! God was speaking to me and reminding me that from the moment I began to pray, and from the moment my family, friends, and congregation began to pray for me, that God heard our prayers and He was sending a response right away!

Sometimes we question if God hears us, if He's really listening to our prayers, and he is! However, the struggle is real. The battle is real, and some answers take time to manifest in our lives. Know this for sure, God has sent your answer!

There was a real spiritual war going on in the heavens just like Daniel experienced. There are times when God sends reinforcements to help fight on your behalf, to make sure the answer to your prayer gets through to you. The key is to have faith and know that God is at work. Go ahead and thank Him for hearing and thank Him for already answering.

I'm not sure where you live, but where I live we have a few interstates that run through the city. At times you can move really quickly from one point to another. Yet there are other times when the traffic is backed up and you just have to wait. You will get to your destination, but it might just take a little bit longer today than it did yesterday. There are times when I have been on flights and the landing was delayed because of the traffic in the air. I always reached my destination, but it might have been just a bit later than the time I wanted to reach it.

So it is in our prayer life. Sometimes there is congestion in the heavens. The battle for your answer is real! God sometimes sends reinforcements to push the answer through because the enemy desires to steal, kill, and destroy your purpose. Just hold on! God is at work on your behalf, and the answer is sure to come. My pastor used to say often that delay does not mean denial. This is so true!

Most Dangerous Prayer To Pray

We used to sing this old song,

> I'll go where You want me to go, dear Lord
> O'er mountain, o'er plain, o'er sea
> I'll say what You want me to say, dear Lord
> I'll be what You want me to be.

Great song, but I'm not sure I have always counted the cost in singing or praying those words.

The most dangerous prayer ever prayed was that of Jesus in the Garden of Gethsemane. As Jesus was "sweating great drops of blood" and as He called upon His Father, the disciples fell asleep. It was in this garden that the defining moment of Jesus' life and ministry took place. The prayer that Jesus prayed was monumental. It was monumental because your salvation and my salvation depended upon Jesus submitting to the Father's will, and not giving into the desire of His humanity to simply walk away from the pain, rejection, and humiliation He was about to experience as He was on the way to His destiny and purpose.

When I was sitting in jail for twelve days I had to come to the understanding that my will had to be submitted to the will of the Father. What if His will was that I stay for months or even five years? What if God's eternal plan doesn't align with my plan? When my will collided with His will, He won.

Jesus' prayer was recorded in Matthew 6:10 (NIV) where He said to the Father, "Your kingdom come. Your will be done, on earth as it is in heaven."

We don't always see the big picture that God sees. I just wanted out of jail, but God wanted to accomplish more than my release. There were lives that God divinely set up for me to love and serve while I was in an uncomfortable situation. I must say that God is not as concerned with our comfort as much as the good news of the Gospel reaching all people, even if it included my discomfort temporarily or long term.

What are you currently facing that is overwhelming you? When all you focus on is the size of your challenge, you'll never see the greatness of God to deliver you. Many times our deliverance from a painful situation is not the goal.

The goal is that you and I are transformed more and more into the image of the risen Savior. The goal is that the character of Christ is revealed through us, and it is most clear when we are going through difficult and painful situations. It is in these moments that the world can see Jesus in us if we submit ourselves to the Father's will.

It's when your focus is the Father's love that you begin to see your deliverance come about. As you focus on the Father's love and purpose for your trial, the size of your challenge will diminish and the size of your God will increase beyond anything you can think or imagine.

Remember that God is for you. Remember that God works all things out for the good of those who love Him and are called by Him. Your testimony is never made without going through fire, challenge, and hardship. You never learn patience and endurance without being put between a rock and a hard place.

As my daughter wrote to me while I was in a most uncomfortable situation, "A testimony can never come without going through a test." Everybody wants a testimony, but nobody wants the test.

There is a real enemy of your soul, the devil. He has plans and schemes to discourage, destroy, and defeat you. One of your most powerful weapons against his schemes is your submission to the Father's will. As you begin to say yes to His will and praise God in your challenge, you will become dangerous to the enemy.

I want to encourage you to be intentional in submitting to the Father's will right now. Why don't you take a moment to pray, and communicate to the Father whatever challenge you are facing. As you talk to Him about your difficulty, also declare to Him that you are fully engaged for His will to be accomplished in this matter. Ask Him to help you see what He sees, that the eternal purposes of the kingdom be fulfilled in your life.

Use this scripture as you pray.

Matthew 6:7–13 (NASB)

"And when you are praying, do not use meaningless repetition as the Gentiles do, for they suppose that they will be heard for their many words. So do not be like them; for your Father knows what you need before you ask Him. "Pray, then, in this way: 'Our Father who is in heaven, Hallowed be Your name. **Your kingdom come. Your will be done**, On earth as it is in heaven. Give us this day our daily bread. And forgive us our debts, as we also have forgiven our debtors. And do not lead us into temptation, but deliver us from evil. For Yours is the kingdom and the power and the glory forever. Amen.'"

Chapter 10

Divine Favor

Daniel 1:9 (NIV): "Now God had caused the official to show favor and compassion to Daniel…"

Daniel 2:14 (NIV): "When Arioch, the commander of the king's guard, had gone out to put to death the wise men of Babylon, Daniel spoke to him with *wisdom and tact.*"

In Japanese culture, admitting guilt or wrong is huge. Humility is huge. The Japanese are a prideful people, and in Okinawa they deal with many Americans because of the military bases located there and we all know that Americans are not the most humble of all creatures. Yet, to show humility can open doors that are doggedly closed.

As I was taken to see the prosecutor for the first time, I was frightened. This whole experience was foreign to me. I've been involved in jail ministry over the years, but I had always been able to leave on my own terms. I had no past experience to help me prepare for meeting the prosecutor, the judge, or the detectives.

As she reviewed my charges, I sat handcuffed to a chair with an English translator close to me. I listened carefully. She did not flinch. She stared me straight in the eyes and was in control of the entire situation. The prosecutor told me that she didn't know who I was, and she was not sure if I might be a terrorist, selling arms, purchasing arms, or involved in some other crime.

While she was speaking, all I wanted to do to was shout that I was innocent of any wrongdoing. But I'm so thankful that I remained silent and just listened to every word she said.

She told me that there are two things in Japan that they absolutely will not tolerate. Those two things are weapons and drugs. She informed me that the only people who have weapons in Japan are the police and the Japanese Mafia.

As a matter of fact, I was stunned that I only saw a few policemen and detectives with a side arm. I did not see one weapon on a police officer inside the jail, or when they would transfer me in a vehicle to the courthouse. Even without firearms, the jail was quiet and orderly.

The moment came when she asked if I would like to make a statement, and this is where I believe the Lord gave me wisdom and would eventually reveal that I had favor with the prosecutor, detectives, and even the judge.

I looked her straight in the eyes and asked her to show me mercy. I apologized that I had offended her and the nation of Japan by my carelessness in packing. I told her that I in no way would ever bring ammunition or a weapon with me into another country, and that I was deeply sorry that I had broken this law. I stressed that I had traveled to Japan for many years, and this was a careless mistake on my part. I once again apologized, and asked that she would show me mercy.

As believers in Jesus, many times we are guilty of sin and offending the Father, yet we try to skirt the issue. We make light of our offense when God simply wants us to come clean, repent, and obey His word.

James reminds us that if we confess our sins to each other we will be healed (James 5:16).

I would find out later that humbling myself, admitting my guilt, and apologizing was huge in my being released. They saw true humility and repentance on my part. It was evident with the guards, detectives, and others that I had favor with them. There was no scheme on my part that they found because I was innocent.

That's exactly how it is with Christ when we repent. The devil (the accuser) tries to lay blame and guilt on us; however, we have gained favor and freedom through our repentance and confession of guilt to Christ. Our crime (sin) has been covered by the blood of Christ.

Too many people walk around seemingly free yet are in chains spiritually because they fail to repent. God is not out to get you! God wants to have communion with you, and He's simply waiting for you to repent, confess, and believe in His Son, Jesus Christ.

There are many who call themselves Christians yet are in chains because they fail to humble themselves and forgive others. You might be a slave to bitterness today because you will not humble yourself before the Lord and confess your bitterness and hurt.

As I walked this particular journey out, the Lord spoke to me that He would give me favor with those who had put me in this jail, but He also told me that He would give me wisdom and tact in communicating with people in author-itative positions.

You may not know me, but my nature is to come unhinged pretty quickly in situations like this. It was remarkable how the Lord gave me calmness and clarity when I would speak to detectives, the prosecutor, the judge, and others.

There is a word that came to Daniel in chapter nine that impacted my life in a powerful way.

Daniel 9:22– 23 (NIV): "He instructed me and said to me, 'Daniel, I have now come to give you insight and under-standing. As soon as you began to pray, a word went out, which I have come to tell you, for you are highly esteemed...'"

"As soon as you began to pray!" This tells me that I should never question whether or not I should lift my request to the Lord. He's anxiously awaiting our requests, and is longing to move on our behalf and for His glory.

The word the angel brought to Daniel was to let him know that he was highly favored by God, and this favor would be like a shield around him.

Let me encourage you right now that you are highly favored of God! He's listening to your requests. Know this moment that "a word has gone out" from the throne room of heaven on your behalf! Orders have been sent. Relief is on the way! Your breakthrough is coming!

As the days began to stack up, I saw the favor of God in my life with the authorities. This scripture out of Daniel was not just something I read about an old character in the

Bible, but it came to life and the favor of God was clearly seen in my situation.

One of the last days of interrogation by the detectives was interesting. The detective I asked to call my wife felt compelled to let me know that he did call her. He brought it up without me asking him. He wanted to assure me that he would not lie to me because he was a good man. It was interesting because he just kept saying it even when I thanked him and told him I appreciated it. It was apparent that my prayers were being answered, and this man's heart was turning with favor toward me.

This detective began to tell me that I was a good person too, because he knew Bishop Whitaker and the people at Zion Christian Fellowship. He wanted me to know that because he knew who Bishop Whitaker was that I had to be a good person like him. He was basically letting me know that he believed now that I didn't really do anything deserving of jail.

I was not interrogated any further by him or by anyone else. It was now just a waiting game for my release. The favor of God was turning the hearts of those in authority towards me. The guards and police officers were friendly to me. It was as if they felt bad that I was in jail.

When I saw the prosecutor for the final time, her attitude and demeanor was one of kindness toward me. As I said earlier, it was as if in my final statements, she was helping me say what needed to be recorded for my good and detailed in their documents.

Ultimate favor was shown when they released me with no fine to pay. That was totally God's favor in my life, and confirmation of a word that was spoken through prayer back in the states that I would do "no time, and pay no fine." That's exactly what happened.

That same favor is at work in your life too. God loves to display His favor in our lives so that we declare His goodness, and so that glory is given to His name so people will know that our God is a loving, powerful God.

Ask God to give you favor with others, and tact in communicating. You will find that your answer to your prayer might get caught up in traffic, but it is for sure to be on the way!

Chapter 11

The Value Of Tests

James 1:2– 4, 12 (NIV): "Consider it pure joy, my brothers and sisters, whenever you face trials of many kinds, because you know that the testing of your faith produces perseverance. Let perseverance finish its work so that you may be mature and complete, not lacking anything. Blessed is the one who perseveres under trial because, having stood the test, that person will receive the crown of life that the Lord has promised to those who love him."

Finding joy in tests and trials is not usually our first response. However, there is always purpose for our pain. Faith produces fruit, but faith can't produce when there is no pressure.

I was raised in Indiana where basketball is king. It seems everywhere you look there is a hoop in somebody's yard, garage, or barn. You just grow up with a love for the game.

A basketball only works when there is the proper pressure in the ball. If there is no pressure in the basketball, it won't bounce. You can't shoot it. It doesn't pass very well. In essence, it has no purpose without some pressure applied. When you put the proper pressure inside the basketball, you can bounce it to a teammate. You can dribble it up the court and shoot it into the hoop.

The pressure in the basketball allows it to bounce properly. So it is in our spiritual lives. Pressure (a test, trial, temptation, struggle) is not meant to destroy us or defeat us. Pressure is meant to expose who we are and our ability to rise to the occasion. When pressure hits your life, what's inside should cause you to bounce back and be useful for God's Kingdom. God desires to see the fruit of perseverance in our lives. He wants us to become mature and complete. It won't happen without experiencing various tests in our life.

I struggled in school when it came to tests. I'm not going to lie. Tests caused me pain. However, as I would study and prepare, the tests became a measuring stick of my growth and knowledge in a particular subject.

Depending on the grade, the test would reveal where I needed improvement and development. The test result would reveal my strengths as well as my weaknesses. It was important for me to not be discouraged about low test scores, but instead to see them as an indicator of my development and a tool to help me grow.

Our spiritual life is filled with tests and examinations. God never puts a test in our way for our failure. He allows tests and struggles to develop us.

This experience in Japan was testing my faith, my view of God, and much more. But this was not my first test, nor will it be my last. The goal is to learn and grow so I am more mature when the next test comes my way because it is definitely coming.

You can never really have a spirit or attitude of perseverance unless you go through a test in life where you have to fight through to get the victory. Yet perseverance is a character trait that should be visible in every believer's life; it allows us to stand during the tests that come our way.

May I go back to basketball? I've watched my oldest son fight through excruciating back pain on the basketball court to finish the game. There have been times when our youngest son has been knocked to the floor while driving to the hoop, and he gets back up to continue the battle on the hardwood. That's perseverance. Playing through the pain to complete the battle.

Spiritually speaking, we have to fight through the pain of disappointments and failures to persevere in the fight of our faith. It doesn't always go smoothly in the Kingdom, but you get up and keep fighting the good fight of faith.

You may have been knocked down by divorce or sickness, but you got back up and persevered through the pain to honor God with your life. You passed the test!

We all fall down, but the key is getting back up through the power of a risen Christ who lives inside of us to keep us on the journey so that we finish the race well.

I would never wish my experience on anyone and I would never want to do it again. However, I'm thankful for what I went through because it revealed what was inside of me, and it produced fruit that was pleasing to God.

James shares good news with us in verse 12 when he writes, "Blessed is the one who perseveres under trial because, having stood the test, that person will receive the crown of life that the Lord has promised to those who love him."

It's difficult to consider ourselves blessed when we're in the midst of the biggest challenge of our life. Yet God says you're blessed.

The greatest rewards for our faithfulness and perseverance are not revealed in this life, but in eternity. Don't get discouraged because you don't see great rewards here and now, but be assured that your rewards are set aside and waiting for you when you hear those words, "Well done, good and faithful servant."

It's through perseverance that we obtain the crown of life. It doesn't come to those who give up, quit, or blame God and others. But it does come to those who persevere through the test.

Chapter 12

Divine Moments In Ordinary Places

Proverbs 16:9 (NLT): "In their hearts humans plan their course, but the Lord establishes their steps."

Proverbs 20:24 (NLT): "A person's steps are directed by the Lord. How then can anyone understand their own way?"

Romans 8:28 (NLT): "And we know that in all things God works for the good of those who love him, who have been called according to his purpose."

Oftentimes when life seems to go crazy, we question God and His existence in our situations. Though we may question where He is, we can be sure that He is always leading and guiding those who trust in Him. Jesus never promised things would be easy. As a matter of fact, Jesus said that we would definitely have trouble in this world, but not to worry because He has already overcome the world.

Always remember that the existence of trouble in your life does not equal the lack of God's presence in our lives. If anything, our trouble assures us of His presence in our lives.

As I flew home from Okinawa, the Lord had another test for me. I didn't sleep from Okinawa to Tokyo and into Denver. I purchased the wifi to communicate with people I hadn't been able to speak with for almost 16 days. It felt good to be back in what had been my normal world.

When I got on my final flight from Denver to Omaha, I was excited. One more short flight, and I would be home. My wife and family would be at the airport, and we were planning a meal at our house together. I was ready.

The plane was small, and my normal aisle or exit row seat wasn't available, which didn't bother me. I was on a plane home.

However, I had the last window seat in the back row of the plane and it was tight. The plane was full, and as I got seated I noticed that there were several rowdy men that were filing onto the plane. They were big, athletic looking men. The loudest of these five or six men realized he was seated on the aisle next to me. This guy was the loudest of them all, and brought with him an adult beverage that he was enjoying.

As we were preparing for takeoff, this guy was punching some of his friends across the aisle, and just being rowdy. Every now and then he would accidentally (or maybe on purpose) bump me. I couldn't understand what he was saying because he was speaking in Spanish. Whatever it was, it was apparently funny. Did I tell you that he was loud?

I just wanted to get home, and this party in the back of the plane wasn't the party I was anxious for.

The plane taxied down the runway and up and away we went. By my calculations we had less than two hours before touch down in Omaha, Nebraska. The Good Life!

So once we got airborne, I put my headphones on and cranked up some Fred Hammond to the delight of my heart. Sure enough this guy bumps me and wants to know what I'm listening to. He asked if he could put my headphones on, and because I really didn't have much choice I let him listen.

It took about ten seconds for him to look at me while literally dropping his drink on the floor. He says, "Momma's music."

I said, 'Excuse me?'

He said, "Momma's music. Are you a Christian?"

Everything changed at this point. Here was the test. Was I too tired, and too busy (really, where was I going 35,000 feet in the air for the next two hours?) to spend time with this man to answer his questions?

I told him I was a Christian and I was also a pastor as well as an artist. When I told him that I wrote and recorded my own music, he wanted to listen to that too. So we listened together for just a few moments and then he wanted to talk with me.

He told me that he and his buddies on the plane were baseball players who missed their original flight in Denver and ended up on my flight. I call this a divine appointment. I should have been on a flight twelve days ago, and they should have been on a flight earlier in this day. This was a God set up.

This man began to share many things about his life. He was married with three children and one on the way. Evidently his lifestyle had been such that he was not proud of the husband and father he had become.

As I listened to him, I just took it all in until he gave me room to speak. I began to share with him that his life was about to change if he would put Jesus first in his life. I told him that God could help him be the father he has always wanted to be and the husband that he desired to be.

You see, we are all just one choice away from life change. One choice is all it takes for us to live the life that God created us to live.

I prayed with him, and when we arrived in Omaha he wouldn't let me off the plane. Literally. Everybody got off the plane, but this guy wanted to know more. He actually told me that he needed me in his life to teach him more about Jesus and about being a husband and father. The plane was literally being cleaned up when we finally exited our seats.

We exchanged phone information and I had the opportunity to meet him again while he was playing in Omaha that week.

My carelessness could have cost this guy the opportunity to receive the love and hope that comes from knowing Christ. I could have had the attitude that I had already been through a lot the past twelve to sixteen days and didn't really have the time or energy to spend with this guy. However, those days in Japan prepared me and reminded me to take advantage of every opportunity to share the love of Christ because we don't know what tomorrow will bring.

Let me just add that God uses everything in our life for His glory and our good. My carelessness landed me in jail for twelve days, but God took that time to prepare me for a baseball player that needed to hear about Jesus.

God doesn't waste or throw away our experiences and act like they did not happen because He desires us to testify and share with others how He delivers, saves, and rescues us.

Today is filled with divine appointments and opportunities from God. No matter what you are going through, don't be careless with the open doors that come your way to give life to those who are seeking for real meaning to their life. Slow down. Listen to those around you, and you will hear the sound of hunger. People all around us are hungry for the truth. What you have freely received, go give it away!

Breathe

My kids bought me an Apple watch for Christmas. I haven't worn a watch on my wrist for 30 years. I don't have a clue how to fully use it. At times I feel like Maxwell Smart trying to use my watch as a phone! Every now and then my watch will vibrate and get my attention. When I look down at my watch it is a pretty teal color with this bold word: BREATHE.

Take a moment and just breathe. Breathe in the blessing of a new day. Breathe in the blessing of your family. Breathe in the goodness of God who gives you another day, another chance, and another opportunity to be a blessing to somebody in your world of influence.

Breathe. Just breathe.

Maybe you would make this daily commitment with me by using 'breathe' as an acronym.

B – be BOLD today

R – REACH out to someone in love today

E – be EXCITED about life

A – choose to have a good ATTITUDE (attitude determines altitude!)

T – TELL somebody they are special and loved

H – HOLD no grudges, bitterness, or resentment toward anyone

E – EXCEL at being YOU; Enjoy who God made you to be. You are one of a kind! Live in the uniqueness that is YOU!

Chapter 13

The Power To Elevate

Isaiah 55:8–9 (NIV): "'For my thoughts are not your thoughts, neither are your ways my ways,' declares the Lord. 'As the heavens are higher than the earth, so are my ways higher than your ways and my thoughts than your thoughts.'"

Many times when we are faced with adversity we are unable to see the big picture. All we can see in front of us is a bad doctor's report, a pink slip, divorce papers, or some other traumatic news that rocks our world. If we can take a step back to catch our breath and look to the Father, we can have a better view of what God might be doing.

If you have ever flown in an airplane you probably have experienced turbulence at different times when you lifted off in a rainstorm or even a snowstorm. It looked terrible outside, and you were probably a little nervous about how the flight would go because of the circumstances—the dark clouds, rain, wind, or snow were all that you could see in front of you.

The awesome thing about planes is they have the power to rise above the clouds and storms to escape the turbulence. By elevating, they pass through the clouds right on up to where the sun is shining. They just need to adjust their altitude by accelerating the massive engines. The power to elevate is already there—it just needs to be accessed and activated.

You and I face storms in our relationships, our finances, and many other areas of our normal lives. Storms arise in our culture that challenge our deepest convictions. When I was 10,000 miles away from home sitting in a cell with Shrek and Donkey, I was in the storm of my life!

Storms are inevitable, but they do not last forever. What we must contemplate is what to do when the storm clouds rise and the lightning seems to be striking all around our lives.

I believe that a transformed mind that exemplifies a Christ-like attitude is the engine or the power that elevates us above the storms that are surely to come our way.

After I took a breath and began to seek God about the dilemma I was in, a transformed mind is what gave me perspective for my situation. I realized that my mind had been in training and in submission to God's word for a life-time, and that I could access His power to lift me above my situation.

Romans 12:1–2 says, "Therefore I urge you brothers and sisters by the mercies of God to offer your bodies as a living sacrifice, holy, acceptable unto God, which is your reasonable service. And do not be conformed to this world but be *transformed by the renewing of your mind* so you can prove what is that good, and acceptable, and perfect will of God."

You and I must learn how to activate and align our thought patterns with Christ when storms come our way so we can elevate our lives above the disturbance. You and I can rise high above the storms of life when we activate the power of Christ within us to align our thoughts with God's thoughts and desires for our lives, which are always higher, wider, and deeper than we could ever imagine or dream of.

The storm is not the issue. The issue is whether we will engage the power within our hearts and minds to stand in agreement with God's view of our situation. The choice is whether or not we will submit ourselves to the mind of Christ, which elevates us, or whether we will crumple into self-pity and doubt, which will allow the storm to over-whelm and destroy us.

Being guilty of having a bullet in my carry-on bag was not the big picture. The fact that less than 1% of Japan's pop-ulation has a relationship with Jesus was the big picture. Shrek and Donkey are the big picture. The prosecutor, detectives, police officers, as well as the judge were in the big picture that God was looking at.

Part of the big picture was God having my full attention to address some personal issues that He wanted to deal with in my life. Personally, I think He could have addressed them well on a white, sandy beach with a cold iced tea within my reach. Once again, God's ways are not our ways!

Would I focus all my energy on my situation, or would I elevate my view to see what God was trying to show me? In short, would I submit to His will? That is the ulti-mate question.

In God's economy, *people are always the big picture*. Every tribe, every tongue, and every nation are continually on the heart of God. And I have learned that He will go to extreme measures to have a representation of Himself to people who have never heard of His goodness.

It's like living in the Midwest, where we have to deal with storms in the spring, storms in the summer, storms in the fall, and storms in the winter. You have to have a mindset that is ready to deal with the storms. You have to prepare and ready yourself for the oncoming storm; it could literally be a life or death scenario if you are not prepared.

To be prepared for the storm means to stock up on food, water, batteries, flashlights, candles, blankets, a generator, and other necessities so that when the storm comes, you simply go to the supplies you have stored up to get you through.

Many individuals who call themselves Christians are destroyed by the storms of life because *they have not prepared themselves* to rise above the storms. They have not stored up God's word in their hearts and minds. Many do not have the word of God hidden in their hearts, so when the storm of temptation comes, they fall prey to the temptation.

Frankly, most Christians operate in their carnal mind and not with a transformed mind that is submitted to Christ.

If you have God's word stored up in your heart and mind, then you can withstand the storm and not be destroyed by its winds. I'm not at all saying you won't question, fear, or struggle with the storm. However, you have everything you need to withstand the impact of life's storms when you hide God's Word in your heart and when you have an ongoing relationship with the Father.

Just like that commercial jet accesses its powerful engines to rise above the turbulence, you and I can choose to access the power that is within us to rise above the various storms of our lives. The power of God is already within you. You simply have to choose to access the power.

The daily disciplines are long gone for many. We feed on 60 second devotionals from the popular voices in the Christian community *instead of building a strong mind and spirit through daily, intentional, strategic personal Bible study, prayer, and meditation on God's Word.* There are no short-cuts to spiritual maturity! A transformed mind comes through the intentional, purposeful, consistent, disciplined life of a believer. That is how a disciple is made.

You cannot prepare for the storm in the middle of the storm. You must be honest that storms are coming, so you must prepare now. No one knows when the storm will come, but we know that it surely will come. Miscarriages, the loss of employment, the deterioration of a marriage, the list goes on and on. Life is filled with storms.

One of the biggest struggles we face when going through challenging situations is not being able to see the bigger picture. I know that it's difficult to see the other side of a test when you're focused on your current situation and position.

Healing is hard to see when your body is dealing with excruciating pain. Yet God's Word says that by His stripes we *were* healed. In God's economy, it's already paid for and manifested. As believers, we are to walk by faith and not by sight. It's difficult to see the sunshine on the other side of the mountain when you're walking through the valley of the shadow of death. I get that. However, if God's word is true in the sunshine, it's true in the storm.

When the one you pledged to love until death parted you decides somewhere along the journey to file for divorce, it's really hard to see reconciliation and healing for your relationship.

I suggest to you that it's in the midst of our darkest experiences in life that the peace, joy, and goodness of God is to be made manifest in our lives to elevate us above our circumstances. The ultimate purpose of this elevation is for God's glory and the enlargement of our vision about who God really is.

Oh, I know that's tough to hold on if you're walking in a dark season right now, but once again, don't doubt in the dark what you know to be true in the light. If truth is only true when life is good, then it is not truth. Truth is truth always, and at all times.

When I walked through this dark event in my life, the only thing on my mind when I heard the words, "You're under arrest," was "GET ME OUT OF HERE NOW!"

Why couldn't they see that I had made an honest mistake? What was the big deal? What I thought was a simple mistake was actually a major violation of Japanese law with serious consequences.

When the U.S. Consul informed me that I should prepare myself to be in jail for a long time, I could not get my mind wrapped around that possibility. I was told plainly that I could spend the next five years in a Japanese prison, and I should come to terms with that real possibility.

In addition, I was told that 99% of all cases that go to trial in Japan, end with conviction. That reality was not comforting to me!

As the days kept passing by and the reality that I wasn't going home soon settled in, I ran across scriptures that began to give me focus and purpose in the midst of my challenge. My hope is that these scriptures will be helpful to you as well.

You see, all I could think about was, "How will my wife deal with my being away for five years?" Our lives were just blessed with our first grandson, and the thought of not seeing him for five years was hard to accept. The enemy of my soul kept attacking my mind with thoughts that I would not see my youngest son until he would have completed his first year of college, which meant I would miss his entire high school experience. Oh, there were many more thoughts that discouraged me and made me question my faith on the deepest levels.

Don't waste your mind on thoughts that destroy, discourage, and decline your faith in God.

You must choose *now* what thoughts you are going to allow to rule your heart and your mind. You see, you need to make decisions now that will rule your heart and mind when trouble hits home. If you wait until trouble comes to determine what you will do, your flesh will win every time.

An Olympian athlete doesn't enter an event without being in shape first. There are years of training and development and preparation for that moment that will determine victory or defeat.

Spiritual training cannot be accomplished in a minute, an hour, or a day. You must commit to spiritual training each and every day so when the moment of struggle and temptation comes you have already decided how you will react to the situation.

1 Corinthians 2:16b (NIV) says, "But we have the mind of Christ."

Wouldn't it be a terrible thing to waste your thoughts on those things that are in direct opposition to the plans and will of God? I was being challenged not to waste my thought life, but instead submit my thoughts and my mind to God and to His will for my life in this situation.

Romans 12:2 (KJV) says, "And be not conformed to this world: but be ye transformed by the renewing of your mind, that ye may prove what is that good, and acceptable, and perfect, will of God."

God wants us to think differently from the world, no matter what circumstance we are facing. His desire is that our mind is renewed and transformed. That's powerful! You need to trade in the old way of thinking and processing in exchange for the new mind that God has for you.

Storms of life can perfect and give us a laser-like focus on the thoughts of God if we choose to direct our thoughts His way.

As I leaned on God's word, something amazing began to take place in my heart and mind. I literally yielded myself to the Lord for whatever He wanted. There was a point about nine days in when I was able to say to the Lord, "If it's Your will for me to go to prison for five years, give me the strength I will need to do it. If there is a purpose that you have for me that requires this journey, I know you'll take care of my family and you'll take care of me."

Believe me when I say that I did not want to stay any longer than the time I had already spent in jail; however, my mind was submitted to whatever God wanted from me. Friend, this was a Garden of Gethsemane moment for me.

"Father, not my will but Yours be done," and I meant it.

What was the point? The point was for me to be completely submitted to the Father. He wants all of me, not just a portion of my life.

God was reminding me that I am not my own, and that I was purchased with the blood of His Son, Jesus. God has a right to use me and move me wherever He chooses, and as a good son I must always remain submitted to the Father's will.

He wanted to know that He had my heart and attention.

Before I move onto the next chapter, allow me to share one last scripture that was important to me.

Isaiah 55:8–9 (NIV): "'For my thoughts are not your thoughts, neither are your ways my ways,' declares the Lord. 'As the heavens are higher than the earth, so are my ways higher than your ways and my thoughts than your thoughts.'"

The ways of God are always higher than our own. How can we fully comprehend the greatness of our God? Yet He invites us to come up higher to where He is.

Jail does not seem like a step up, but a major step down! However, the Kingdom doesn't operate as the world does.

I have heard many testimonies throughout the years about how God allowed people to be in prison and terrible situations that ultimately put them in a place to share the Gospel with people who had never heard, or even for just one person to hear the Gospel.

There were other men in jail with me who needed to see Jesus, and I was a representative of the King. There were a host of police officers, investigators, a judge, translators, guards, a prosecutor, along with friends and family, who needed to see Jesus in action in my life. My prayer is that I was faithful to represent Him so others could know Him as I do.

The higher purpose was being able to communicate to the men in my cell that Jesus loved them. I didn't speak a word of Japanese, but through a variety of ways, they saw Jesus in me.

My home church and friends around the world were impacted by my setback. God drew them to a deeper place of prayer and unity as a body of believers, and this was part of His higher plans.

I believe that God did even more than we asked because when people are praying in the Spirit they are praying in complete agreement with the Father, and I believe God even allowed my situation to draw people to pray in the Spirit for situations they may never know about.

God has higher plans! God has higher purposes! We must align our thoughts and our will to His higher purposes even if it costs us our comfort and pleasure. In order for me to see the deeper and higher things of God, it required that I let go of immature thinking, selfishness, and my desires.

Christianity is not safe! Christianity is not about escaping uncomfortable situations. Jesus' life was an example to us, and if we are to share in His glory, we must also share in His sufferings. That's a part of the Gospel that just doesn't preach well in America, but it is inescapable.

I don't know about you, but I want to climb into the higher realms of Godliness so our world will see what a true follower of Jesus looks like. There may be pain and discomfort involved, but His promises will carry me through. To reach the heights that God desires us to live in requires letting go of the temporal for what is eternal. This exchange must take place in order to go higher.

If you will align your thought life to the word of God, you will find that God will take your setbacks and turn them into incredible comebacks for your good and for His glory!

The prophet Isaiah writes again in chapter 40 and verse 31 (NIV) some powerful words to us: "But those who hope in the Lord will renew their strength. They will soar on wings like eagles; they will run and not grow weary, they will walk and not be faint."

It's interesting to view the eagle. Eagles can see small prey up to two miles away. They can even change their altitude when they see a storm coming their way. Eagles climb higher to rise above the storm.

You and I can climb above our storms and challenges as we train ourselves to understand that God has higher and greater purposes for our lives.

You will be tested! You will face difficult challenges both now and in the future! As you wait and hope upon the Lord, you will rise above the storm to see the greater plan that God has for you.

I could not imagine the massive prayer movement that was going on while I was in my "extended stay" facility in Okinawa. Friends from West Africa, Spain, Japan, and throughout America were praying for me. It excites me to know that God was doing great things in the hearts and lives of people around the world all while he was working out my release date.

You can't see the greater plan if you are consumed with yourself. You will never see God's greater purposes if you can only seek Him for a temporal blessing.

One of the keys to my climbing higher to see that God had greater purposes for me was acknowledging that I had to "drop some weight." Now I know what you're thinking, but I'm not talking about physical weight. I had to get rid of some thought processes and other attitudes of my heart that were keeping me in the lowlands.

If you're going to climb higher and see more than you see now, you'll need to get rid of some mindsets that keep you in the lowlands. Negative thoughts and self-pity will destroy your life.

Stop focusing on "Why me, Lord?" Don't get angry with God when He doesn't answer your prayer in your way or in your timing. Ask God, "What's Your will in this matter? Help me to see what you see and what you want to do, Father!'"

Romans 12:1 reminds us that our mind must be transformed through the Word of God, which allows us to see beyond our challenge to the bigger plans of God.

If we remain in our carnal thoughts, we can only see and feel our pain. If we allow God to transform our mind, we are able to see His picture and the lives He wants us to impact for His glory.

The purpose of the pain in your storm is to reveal more of who God is. Our pain is meant for our good, and ultimately for God's glory. In the midst of your trouble and your trial, God is inviting you to climb higher to a level of faith that causes you to see the big picture of His will and His plans.

As I close this chapter, allow the Holy Spirit to reveal to you the weight of attitudes and mindsets that hinder you from elevating to new heights in your faith. Be encouraged that beyond the storm clouds of your life, the Son is shining. He is always shining.

Chapter 14

The Value Of Friendship

P roverbs 27:6 (KJV): Faithful are the wounds of a friend; but the kisses of an enemy are deceitful.

Proverbs 27:17 (KJV): Iron sharpeneth iron; so a man sharpeneth the countenance of his friend.

"Now it came about when he had finished speaking to Saul, that the soul of Jonathan was knit to the soul of David, and Jonathan loved him as himself. Saul took him that day and did not let him return to his father's house. Then Jonathan made a covenant with David because he loved him as himself. Jonathan stripped himself of the robe that was on him and gave it to David, with his armor, including his sword and his bow and his belt. So David went out wherever Saul sent him, and prospered; and Saul set him over the men of war" (1 Samuel 18 NASB).

This is one of the most amazing descriptions of friendship we see throughout the Bible. Jonathon is the son of the king, and David has been anointed to be king. It Is a complex situation, but Jonathon and David's friendship is deeper than the complicated lives they are living.

David has recently gained fame for killing a giant named Goliath, and King Saul is not excited to have someone else receive praise and adulation that exceeds his own. It gets so bad that David is running for his life, living in caves to protect himself from the attacks of the king. Jonathon goes to David's defense before his father King Saul, and he protects David from being killed.

Life sometimes gets really ugly, confusing, and complicated for all of us. We face jealousy from family and friends when we see a level of success that might exceed others. You see, not everybody wants to see you succeed or celebrate your success.

We often jump to conclusions that end up damaging relationships for extended periods of time, and sometimes for the remainder of our lives.

Proverbs 17:17 (NIV) says, "A friend loves at all times, and a brother is born for a time of adversity."

When I found myself in a jail cell in Okinawa, Japan, I was distraught and needed a friend. The first person who came to see me was Bishop Whitaker's son, Joshua. I cannot describe what I experienced when I saw him. This young man was like the awesome beauty of a sunrise coming up over the ocean. He encouraged me and assured me that he would do everything in his power to help me get released.

The first thing Joshua told me was this: "Pastor Booth, I'm going to treat this situation like you are my own father. I will not quit until we get this resolved."

It paralleled the situation when Jesus said, "If you've seen Me, you've seen the Father." I saw Bishop's face, and I heard Bishop's voice when Joshua spoke those words. I knew I was in good hands. I knew that everything would be done to assure my release. I was still concerned, but I knew that God was at work. My heart was eased with the kindness, love, and concern that I saw with Joshua.

Joshua was in communication almost daily with my son, Jevan, and I think they have a bond today that can never be broken because of the journey they shared over those twelve days.

I would find out that friends in Spain, Burkina Faso, the U.S., Japan, and other places were praying for me. It was overwhelming and comforting to have the friendship of people all around the world focusing their prayers on my family and me.

Not only did I experience the friendship of people but I also experienced the friendship of Jesus. He was with me. He was experiencing this whole situation with me. He was never going to leave me. He was present in the midst of my difficulty.

We used to sing this song, "What a Friend We Have in Jesus," when I was a young boy. The lyrics comforted me:

> What a friend we have in Jesus,
> All our sins and griefs to bear!
> What a privilege to carry
> Everything to God in prayer!
> Oh, what peace we often forfeit,
> Oh, what needless pain we bear,
> All because we do not carry
> Everything to God in prayer!
> Have we trials and temptations?
> Is there trouble anywhere?
> We should never be discouraged—
> Take it to the Lord in prayer.

Can we find a friend so faithful,
Who will all our sorrows share?
Jesus knows our every weakness;
Take it to the Lord in prayer.
Are we weak and heavy-laden,
Cumbered with a load of care?
Precious Savior, still our refuge—
Take it to the Lord in prayer.
Do thy friends despise, forsake thee?
Take it to the Lord in prayer!
In His arms He'll take and shield thee,
Thou wilt find a solace there.

Sometimes it's when you go through a storm that you realize how close Jesus is to you. The truth of the matter is that His closeness never changes! We just draw near to Him more when we are going through storms.

Friendships are vital to the life of every believer. God never intended for us to live out our lives alone. David had Jonathon. Moses had Aaron. Jesus had Peter, James, and John as well as the other disciples.

There are at least 59 references to "one another" in the New Testament of the Bible. You and I are meant to love one another, bear one another's burdens, pray for one another, be at peace with each other, forgive one another, and much more. We can't experience "one another" unless we develop friendships that go deeper than surface-level conversations.

I have experienced betrayal in my journey of life. There are times when I have experienced people letting me down and gossiping about me. Regardless, I will continue to develop life-long friendships. I will make myself vulnerable and transparent to others so that when true friends are needed, they will be revealed as I go through whatever adversity I am experiencing.

On the other hand, I also want to *be* that friend who is available when adversity hits someone close to me. I want to be that friend who celebrates the joys, experiences, and successes that might exceed my own successes in life.

How our world would change if we focused on developing healthy friendships. If you desire to have close friends, you must make yourself friendly to others.

Proverbs 18:24 (KJV) says, "A man that hath friends must shew himself friendly: and there is a friend that sticketh closer than a brother."

Be encouraged to put yourself out there and develop friendships that will be your comfort, encouragement, and support when life deals you a difficult hand.

Would you take time to pray and search your heart for friendships that might need your attention? You may need to call or visit someone to ask forgiveness.

Ask the Lord for His help in developing relationships that honor Him, and that allow you to experience the fullness that comes from being in relationship with another human being.

Life is short, and I know there are some relationships that won't fully heal because it takes two for that to happen. Just be responsible for what you have control over. You can choose to forgive. You can choose to live in today and for the future, and not live in the past for what could have been. The past has taken place, but the future is yet to be seen.

Will you be a friend? Will you love others unconditionally? Will you choose to be a friend for another during a time of their trials?

I'm still working on this relationship thing. And I am forever grateful for the friendships that God has provided for me, especially in my time of adversity.

Chapter 15

Letters From Home

My wife and I were married in 1982, and we were excited about our new lives together. One of our dreams was to start a family of our own. The plans we had took some detours as we suffered miscarriages during our first seven years of marriage. It was difficult for us when all of our friends were starting to have children.

I remember when Terri found out she was pregnant again and needed to have some bed rest. My mom came over with one of her friends and prayed over my wife and the child she was carrying, and we just knew that this time we would welcome a little boy or little girl into our world.

Sure enough, on October 23, 1988, our dream came true with the birth of our daughter Jordan Elizabeth. She was our miracle baby, and she was the center of our lives. Our desire was to see her grow up to know Jesus and live out her God-given purpose and destiny.

Following Jordan, we were blessed with two sons, Jevan and Jackson. We were having the time of our life with our kids. They were all different, and they brought much joy to our lives.

Fast forward to 2000 when we made our move to Omaha. Our family was complete, and we were going strong in our new ministry. We honestly felt satisfied with our family, and we were now both about forty years of age.

God has a way of jumping right into the middle of life, and He surprised us with another boy in 2002. Jadin came into our world and brought another measure of joy to our lives that we couldn't imagine without him.

We have the joy of our children joining us for ministry in many nations around the world as well as their involvement in our local church ministry in Omaha. They love being a part of seeing people come to know Jesus, and that is one of the greatest joys of our lives.

When I found myself far away from home in a jail cell without any idea of when I would return to my family, my heart was saddened for my children who had to go through this because of my carelessness.

I couldn't call them, and they couldn't call me. Not being able to hear my wife or my children's voices for over twelve days was one of the most difficult things I've ever experienced. When I was released and I made that call to my wife, I cannot explain what emotions ran through me when I simply heard her voice. It was exhilarating and brought me such happiness to just hear her call my name and tell me she loved me.

On about day five or six of my incarceration, I was told that I had some mail that they were going to allow me to read after they examined it. Joshua Whitaker had been able to receive e-mails from my family and friends, and then he gave them to the police to review and give to me.

The first e-mail that was printed off for me to read was from my daughter. I could hardly get through it as the tears were streaming down my face. The little, spunky, beautiful girl that my wife and I raised was now a young married woman with a husband and son of her own.

This precious little girl that came into our lives as a gift from God was now encouraging me with the same word we had sown into her life as long as she was in our home.

3 John 1:4 said exactly how I felt when I read Jordan's e-mail: "I have no greater joy than to hear that my children are walking in the truth."

Jordan shared some encouraging words with me, and then she told me that the Lord had given her this scripture to share with me from Isaiah 40:28–31 (NASB): "Do you not know? Have you not heard? The Everlasting God, the Lord, the Creator of the ends of the earth does not become weary or tired. His understanding is inscrutable. He gives strength to the weary, and to him who lacks might, He increases power. Though youths grow weary and tired, and vigorous young men stumble badly, yet those who wait for the Lord will gain new strength; they will mount up with wings like eagles, they will run and not get tired, they will walk and not become weary."

My heart was filled with joy as I read this scripture and the note that Jordan wrote me. There was a sense of fulfillment that my daughter was not falling apart but was gaining strength from God's word and was encouraging me with the same. She wanted me to know that everything was going to be all right. She encouraged me to stay strong and not give up because God was going to release me soon.

As I read her words, it solidified a confidence within me that God was in control and that more was happening than I was totally aware of.

Once again, I realized that God's ways and purposes are much higher than I could reach. He had plans that were way beyond my simply being released. He was working deep in the hearts of my children. What was planted over the years began to reveal a harvest that made my heart glad.

My son-in-law, Lucas, reminded me to remain in prayer and the word. He also shared some reminders from our good friend Dr. Prince Parker, who said, "It is important to pray in the Spirit. I may not know what my brothers are going through around the world, but the Spirit who is in them is also in me, and the Spirit knows exactly what they are going through, exactly where they are, and exactly what they need. I've taken comfort in that we may not have all the answers and we may not know what you're going through, but the Spirit knows, and we are joined through the same Spirit in believing with you!"

This is a great reminder of the power of praying in the Spirit, and how much more can be done than we realize because the Spirit of God is at work.

Lucas concluded with three important essentials that we learned through David Ravenhill.

1. The Presence of God is always with us, according to Matthew 28:20, Deuteronomy 31:6, and Colossians 1:2.
2. The Passion of God's love for me is everlasting, according to Jeremiah 31:3 and John 3:16.

3. The Power of God is at work and will complete God's desires, according to Ephesians 3:20.

These were vitally important for me to be reminded of and stand upon until I was released.

My oldest son Jevan wrote me and wanted me to know that he had everything under control at home, so I didn't need to worry. My favorite words of encouragement came through his many conversations with Joshua, when Jevan had some specific instructions for me. See, he knows his father all too well, and let's just say my temperament is not naturally one of patience and long-suffering.

Joshua met with me one day and shared some of the e-mails with me, and when we were almost done he kind of laughed and smiled to say that Jevan had one more message for me. The message was short and sweet, and it was exactly what I needed to hear. Jevan said, "Tell my dad to be cool, calm, and collected."

I was crying before Joshua told me this, and after he told me, I could not stop laughing. Those instructions fit Jevan to a T—short, precise, and pointed instructions that he knew his dad needed. And by the way, it wouldn't necessitate his writing it down because it was easy to repeat! Man, I needed his message, and I needed the laugh.

When I finally made it home, I was told how at different times my wife would be struggling or one of my other kids were having a hard day, and it was Jevan who calmed things down and brought perspective to the situation. I'm glad he is who he is. I was proud of the way he led our home and was strong for his mother and siblings during this time of testing.

My son Jackson works for the State Department in Washington, D.C., and when he found out about my predicament, he was able to catch a flight home to be with the family.

Jackson wrote me and shared a scripture that one of the elders, Bill Purnell, had shared in one of the prayer meetings. It was Psalm 121:1-8, and I would like to share it with you because I believe you need to be encouraged by the power of God's word right now.

> I lift up my eyes to the mountains – where does my help come from? My help comes from the Lord, the Maker of heaven and earth. He will not let your foot slip- he who watches over you will not slumber; indeed, he who watches over Israel will neither slumber nor sleep. The Lord watches over you- the Lord is your shade at your right hand; the sun will not harm you by day, nor the moon by night. The Lord will keep you from all harm-he will watch over your life; the Lord will watch over your coming and going both now and forevermore. (NIV)

What a powerful reminder to us of the God that we serve. He's not sleeping while you're suffering! He's fully aware of your circumstance and is at work even when it seems He is silent! God is worthy of praise because He is faithful and true to His word about you and me.

I pray that passage of scripture strengthens your heart this very moment.

My youngest son, Jadin, wrote to let me know how much he missed me, which tore me up all over again. He had me smiling, though, when he wrote that he had shaved for the first time! I was excited to get back and see him, along with the rest of my family. Their words encouraged me and kept me focusing on positive thoughts.

One special e-mail came from a little boy in our church named Trey. Trey just wanted to send me a picture of himself wearing our Freedom Run 5K t-shirt. It was such a blessing to know that he was thinking of me, and his family was praying for me.

I received many e-mails of encouragement from various people, but my wife's e-mails were always my favorites. She always let me know they were okay, and she would tell me about the powerful prayer meetings that were taking place at Freedom Worship Center Omaha.

This strengthened me so much! I often say to our congregation that a PRAYING CHURCH is a POWERFUL CHURCH! They were living it out and I was experiencing the power of God because of all the prayer that was taking place in Omaha and around the world.

My mother is a mighty prayer warrior, and her church in Indiana was praying for me regularly. She sent word through one of the e-mails that one of the men in the church heard God say to him in prayer, "No fine and no time!"

That is exactly what happened. I was released, and when I asked what my fine was, they looked at me and said, "There is no fine." God is good!

These letters from home were a true lifeline of faith, hope, and encouragement to me. I hope they encouraged you as well.

Chapter 16

Final Post

I t's amazing how we plan our lives and then life takes an unexpected turn that sometimes shakes us to our core. My plan was to visit Bishop Whitaker for a few days to encourage him and return home, just like I had done six or seven times before. No big deal. At least that's how I planned it.

We serve a God who was not surprised at all by what took place in my life, and He is not surprised at what is going on in your life as you read my story. I know that He will see you through, and you will learn the valuable lessons that you need to learn.

As I boarded my flight home and found my seat, my plan to sleep vanished quickly—so many thoughts were running through my head! I actually began writing this book on the return flight to Omaha.

For the next fourteen to fifteen hours I wrote my thoughts down, and I had an amazing conversation with a lady seated next to me who had just spent the prior two weeks as a speech therapist to children in the Phillipines who just received a cleft pallet surgery. I was taken in by what she had the privilege of being a part of. She was giving children a new life as they had been blessed with this surgery and as she worked with their speech development.

You knew it would happen, though. She asked me where I had been and what I had been doing. The look on her face was priceless when I told her I was just released from jail in Okinawa! I thought for a minute she would call a stewardess to reseat her, but to my surprise she wanted to know every detail. So this was the first time I told my story, and she was speechless.

Maybe this will be the one and only book I write, but I wanted to close with a Facebook post that I wrote on the flight home on Saturday, April 23, 2016.

> Hey everybody! Good news! I made it through security this time by the grace of God and I'm coming home! Hard to put into words what the last 16 days have been like. The first news I heard in twelve days included a couple of earthquakes in mainland Japan with tsunami warnings, Prince's death, and Steph Curry's ankle injury. I've been without connection to the world for a while and need to get caught up. I just want to say a huge THANK YOU to everyone who has been praying for me and my family during this time. God has answered your prayers! I must tell you that God answered your prayers the day your prayer was on your lips, but traffic has been pretty heavy in this part of the world (Daniel 10). I must believe that your prayers accomplished much more than helping me come home, though. God always does more, and maybe He used this situation to engage many praying in the Spirit together to advance His Kingdom in ways we don't yet know. Much to tell, and

much more to be thankful for. I'm thankful for friends and my Freedom Family. I'm also thankful for my Booth, Bowman, Grimes, Justice, and Trujillo family. I am so proud of how Jordan, Lucas, Jevan, Jackson, and Jadin stepped up in their faith to trust God. He who finds a wife finds a good thing, and finds favor from the Lord (Proverbs 18:22). Wow! Did I marry way up! I love you, Terri! Love my family!!! I hope to see many of you at FWC this Sunday. God has been amazing to me. I'll leave you with this and say goodnight from 35,000 feet somewhere over the Pacific: *Don't ever doubt in the dark what you know to be true in the light. God is good. All the time, God is good.* May He receive all the glory from my life that He rightly deserves. See you soon. #Psalm121 #Isaiah54:17 #Isaiah7:9b